Roots and Shoots
Ursulines of the Roman Union England
1923-2023

Acknowledgements

With special thanks to Sister Angela Cronin who painted the flame at the beginning of each chapter and to Paula Vaughan who designed the cover of this book and offered invaluable advice on publication.

This project would not have been possible without access to the Ursuline archives, both here and in Rome. We thank Sister Katharine Glencross, Our English Archivist. Emanuele Lauro, archivist in Rome and Shirley Ward for access to the Wimbledon archives.

We are also specially indebted to Therese Smith O.B.A and Denis Smith. We were only able to embark on this project after Therese's retirement from St Bonaventure's when they indefatigably catalogued the extensive archives housed at Forest Gate.

We acknowledge the use of the following:

Websites
Generalate website, Rome- https://ursulines-roman-union.org/en/
French Province- https://ursulines.union.romaine.catholique.fr/
Irish Ursulines- https://www.ursulines.ie/

Publications
Ursulines in England 1851-1981- Mother Winefride Sturman
Sister Mary Angela Boord - Mother Winefride Sturman
The Ursulines Greenwich 1877-1977
Ursuline Convent Wimbledon 1892-1992- Avey Pounder

Artwork
The image of St Angela used in the Last Word, from Péreire, Paris.
Artwork commissioned for the appointment of Headteacher Fiona Stone. Created by Year 7-9 students and led by Mr Ray Butler, Head of the Art department.

Proofreading
Thank you to Mrs Catrina Hamilton, Fidelma Boyd, Sr Vianney Connolly and Emily Barron for their help and encouragement.

Contents

CHAPTER 1 — OUR ROOTS
St Angela's life and The Company she founded
Her influence on education and the beginnings of Ursuline education

CHAPTER 2 — EMERGING ROMAN UNION
The beginning of the Roman Union in 1900 when the then Pope recommended this now worldwide group of independent convents join together in Rome.
Not everyone did so, as there were already pre-existing groups that wished to remain and others that preferred to be diocesan

CHAPTER 3 — OUR ENGLISH PROVINCE
In the early 1900's anticlerical laws made it illegal to teach religion in French schools so many convents took refuge in England. Some had already fled here earlier from Germany. At the same time, many Irish sisters were joining English Convents so from its outset the English Province had a very international mix.

CHAPTER 4 — OUR MISSIONS
The 20th Century was a time of great Missionary influence in the Church and the "Roman Union" became very central in this. So here, we have recorded the names of all sisters who went on the Missions and the Missionary awareness of our schools

CHAPTER 5 — FIRMLY ROOTED- URSULINES 1923 VATICAN 2
By the early 20th Century convent schools had 50 years of experience in England and had made a significant mark on English education especially for women. This section deals with that development and history especially immediately post the Second World War. There are also articles from past students. These have been chosen to cover all our schools

CHAPTER 6 — SHAKEN TO OUR ROOTS VATICAN II 2023
This section deals with the many changes that occurred in parishes and convents post Vatican II. Through the personal accounts of each sister living today, we have tried to reflect our convent life in the 21st Century. Topics have been chosen to cover our wide range of activities

CHAPTER 7 — EVENTS AND PEOPLE
Here we have sampled a varied collection of events, of personal, or historical significance, that have had a marked effect in shaping our lives as Ursulines

CHAPTER 8 — EMBRACING OUR FUTURE
In this our final chapter we have addressed the re-shaping of our lives according "to times and circumstances" as wisely recommended by St Angela and the steps we have taken to leave a clear legacy

Key Dates:

Foundations | | Closures
Forest Gate	1862	-
Greenwich	1877	2023
Wimbledon	1892	-
Westgate	1904	2021
Crewe	1907	1933
Ilford	1943	-
Christ's College	1964	1980
Bickley	1978	1986
Shotton	1980	2015
Lourdes Care Home	1985	2021
Silvertown/Beckton	1989	1995
Lancaster	1993	2015
Surrey Docks	1994	2000
Wythenshawe	1994	2015
Catford	2008	2016

Other dates

Birth of St Angela	1474
Foundation of the Company	1535
Greenwich Missionaries leave for Australia	1882
Birth of the Roman Union	1900
English Province Beginnings	1923
Missions	1927
WWII	1939
Greenwich Bombed	1941
Education Act	1944
Vatican II	1962
Formation of Serviam, our Lay Association	1984
Ursuline Links	2010
London Olympics	2012
Ursuline Education Community	2019

Foreword

What caused you to pick up this book? Maybe you have an Ursuline relative or went to an Ursuline school? Maybe you taught in one of the schools? Maybe the attractive cover caught your eye? Whatever it was, you are in for a treat.

This volume gives you an insight into the lives and work of Roman Union Ursuline sisters living in England. This is not a history book, though historical facts are to be found. You will be introduced to St Angela Merici, the small 16th Century Italian woman who established a Company which can be found today in every continent. Her wise words continue to inspire us.

As you read you will be drawn into the lives of women who, faithful to their religious calling, did their best to spread the good news of Jesus' message. In 1923 the Ursulines were well established in England and fully engaged in schools either teaching or in supportive roles. Through their schools they had been making a significant contribution to women's education in this country.

As the years went by "according to times and circumstances" as St Angela had sensibly said, other ministries emerged where the sisters could use their gifts and talents. In the pages that follow you will find a snapshot of sisters, who, like their predecessors, made efforts to bring about change for the good of others.

The book makes clear the richness of belonging to an international organisation. Our lives and those of our students are enhanced by visits to and from many lands. Our many missionaries have been courageous and generous.

As we look to the future we do so with courage and gratitude. Ursuline numbers in England are small, yet St Angela's charism lives on in the staff and students in our schools, the young adults engaged in Ursuline links and the many women who have been inspired by the Serviam ideal.

Sr. Una McCreesh and Elizabeth Durrant have woven a rich and attractive tapestry of lives well lived in the service of others. They have enabled people to come alive on the page and allowed each one's story to inspire the reader.

Sister Kathleen Colmer OSU

Our Roots

Our First Steps

We could not begin to discuss our history and achievements without first introducing a woman, without whom none of it would be possible. We must go back to 15th Century Italy to the small town of Brescia, where our Founder Angela Merici was born. She was a woman of prayer, caught up with the love of Christ. She had a heart that was open to solving the social problems of her time; her contagious serenity was a sign of balance and peace at a time of unrest. Known as 'La Madre', she drew love and respect from those around her and from all levels of society. As Ursulines, we try to follow her example in all that we do.

Saint Angela's Story 1474-1540

Angela Merici was born in Desenzano, a town on Lake Garda Italy, in 1474. Soon after her birth, the family moved out of town to their farm at Le Grezze, a few miles away. Here Angela became familiar with the rhythms of country life. Each night the family gathered and her father would read to the children about the lives of the saints, and these stories influenced Angela throughout her life.

However, around 1490, her parents and elder sister died and she went, probably with her younger brother, to live with her uncle Biancosi in Salò. Here, life was more sophisticated but she continued to live very simply. It likely in Salò that Angela became a Franciscan Tertiary. This is an organisation still existing today that enables people to live by the spirit of St Francis, while continuing with their ordinary lives.

After some time she returned to the house at Le Grezze (*right*) and stayed here roughly 20 years. In 1516, while she was still living there, her Franciscan superiors asked her to go to Brescia to help Caterina Patengola, a friend of their community, who had lost her husband and children. Whilst there, she met Antonio Romano, a friend of Caterina's nephew. She would later live in his large house as a 'spiritual mother' for 14 years.

During her time in Brescia, Angela welcomed all who came to her for help; those seeking her prayer or her practical advice. She had a particular gift for enabling groups, or families, who had long-standing disputes to be reconciled with each other; wealthy lords, theologians, preachers and the ordinary people of the city, would seek her out. So, Brescia now became her home. When the city was under threat of invasion, she went with Agostino Gallo and his family to Cremona. On their return she lived for some months with Agostino's family in front of the Church of San Clemente.

Angela soon became aware of the young women who were looking for a life of consecration without the need to enter a monastery, and she felt called by God to create something new in the Church for them. In the last years of her life, she moved to a room by the Church of St Afra. It was here that she founded her new Company of St Ursula which is still, today, the active headquarters of the company she founded, now known as 'Angelines'. St Angela's body is preserved on an altar here.

Varallo Shrine

The 16th Century was a time when going on pilgrimage to Holy places was a deep expression of Faith. In 1524, Angela went to the Holy Land on pilgrimage with her cousin Biancosi and Antonio Romano. On the journey she temporarily lost her sight and saw the holy places with the eyes of her heart. The next year she went to Rome for the Holy Year, a year of jubilee held every 25 years to the present day. Here she had an audience with Pope Clement VII who invited her to remain in Rome and continue her good works, but this was not where she felt God was calling her. She also went twice to Varallo in Italy where there was a newly opened shrine showing the life of Christ, in 45 chapel-like enclosures each with life sized terracotta figures. Today it is a UNESCO site.

Angela had a deep faith and felt drawn to Jesus whom she sought and found everywhere. 'Everywhere' for her meant long hours of prayer; it also meant every place where she felt she had a task to do, every person she met, every service she rendered according to needs and circumstances. Active and devoted lay people found in her an inspiring leader, deeply faithful to the Church. In the family home at Le Grezze, which is still standing today, one can see that she lived very simply and was available to the people around her. Her presence is still very much alive in the present Le Grezze parish church of St Angela Merici nearby.

The Foundation of the Company of St Ursula

With the foundation of the Company of Saint Ursula, in Brescia, northern Italy, in 1535, Saint Angela Merici offered the young women of her day an alternative to religious life and an enclosed monastery in the cloister. It was a most daring initiative for the time.

Like nuns, the members of the Company offered themselves as consecrated spouses of the Son of God, but without vows and while living in their own homes and continuing their work. The form of government of the Company was lay and female, making known to society Angela's confidence in a woman's ability to discern, to judge for herself and to govern herself.

After Angela's death, Companies were founded in several cities in Italy, with Rules more or less the same as the Company of Brescia. Gradually the members of these Companies came to live together and in answer to a need of the times, they were often asked to teach in the schools of Christian Doctrine, set up after the Council of Trent (1545-1563) to combat religious ignorance.

Beginning of the Order of St Ursula

Angela's charism is like a root with many branches and is expressed also in the form of religious congregations.

In France, towards the end of the 16th century, a Company was begun by a group of young women in Avignon. Other companies sprang up quickly in different parts of France. But, by the beginning of the 17th century, following the decrees of the Council of Trent, many communities, for a variety of reasons, chose to become convents with cloisters and vows. The first was in Paris in 1612. This was the beginning of the Order of St Ursula. The Ursuline way of life had changed, but the sisters continued their ministry of teaching Christian doctrine. St Angela's ideal of a life of prayer and action remained but took on a different form and her ministry lived on but in a different form. This transition to monastic life was a major turning point. It gave rise to a great flowering of spirituality and also led to an incredible expansion of the Ursuline Order. At the end of the 17th century, in France, there were 300 Ursuline convents.

Ursuline Convents in France in the 17th Century

St Ursula: The Legend

Stained glass window in the chapel at Lourdes Care Home, Westgate-on-Sea

Angela Merici chose to put her new company under the protection of the early English saint, St Ursula; a saint popular in the Middle Ages as the Patroness of Learning. It was a particularly appropriate choice, as it reflected St Angela's concern for the development and fulfilment of young women.

Historical evidence of St Ursula's life has been lost to time but the relationship between St Angela and St Ursula remains strong.

Ursula was the daughter of a Christian King in Britain in the 4th Century. She was asked to marry the son of a King from a much larger and more powerful kingdom. Ursula agreed, on the condition that her husband converted to Christianity and that they would go on Pilgrimage together. The Prince agreed.

Ursula and her entourage of maidens and her husband to be, began their pilgrimage to the Holy Land. During the journey, strong winds blew them off course and they arrived in Cologne. Whilst there, Ursula had a dream that they would all be martyred on their return. Undaunted by this dream, she prepared her companions for martyrdom. They were murdered by the Huns in Cologne for refusing marriage and faced their death with great courage and faith.

In the time when St Angela lived, the legend of St Ursula would have been widespread and popular. St Ursula would have captured Angela's imagination as a young woman of deep faith. And so, she placed her company under the patronage of St Ursula, a virgin and a martyr.

Birth of the Roman Union

Roman Union Beginnings

The formation of the Company of St Angela in 1535 was a ground breaking initiative both, in its concept and structure. But St Angela with 'feminine intuition and wisdom' was aware that life is shaped by multiple factors and wisely said, *"If according to times and circumstances the need arises to make new rules or do something differently do it prudently and with good advice"*. The formation of the Ursuline order, which was shaped by key events, but particularly by the Council of Trent, has always remained faithful to the spirit of St Angela, their unquestioned foundress.

As we have seen, by the end of the 17th century there were over 300 Ursuline convents in France. St Mary of the Incarnation had already established a thriving foundation in Canada and rapid development continued throughout Europe and the rest of the world. By the 19th Century Ursuline convents were to be found on all five continents.

Throughout this time, there were many calls for greater unity and indeed in France the development of Congregations, that is "regional families" founded from one source and sharing the same constitutions were a form of union. However, each community remained autonomous, elected its superior, trained its own novices and was subject to the local bishop.

By the 19th century two events gave increasing urgency to the call for unity. On 24th May 1807, St Angela was canonised and the Ursuline convent in Rome became a focal point for Ursulines worldwide. The fall of the Papal States in 1870 meant that convents in Italy were in danger of closure. There was already considerable networking among Ursuline Convents in different countries and continents and Rome. A little later Calvi also in Italy, appealed to France for help. The Convent in Blois, France responded to this plea offering financial and moral support.

The final catalyst was a wish expressed by Pope Leo XIII to see all the Ursulines united under the authority of one Superior General living in Rome. This recommendation was sent to all the Ursulines and the bishops of their dioceses concerned, inviting them to consider forming a Union. 71 superiors and delegates responded and voted on the plan for a General Government. 62 of the monasteries joined the Union. There was a sense of urgency and verbal approval of the Holy Father was sought and given.

On 28th November 1900, The Roman Union was born and was followed by the first General Chapter where delegates met in Rome.

Organisation of the Roman Union

There was likely to have been disappointment that this Chapter was unable to tackle some of the weightier problems of finance and that houses remained autonomous under a bishop. However, two apparently small changes were achieved which were to prove very effective.

The new name ROMAN UNION was chosen to assert its international character from the very beginning. It was thus totally distinguishable from the many other varying Ursuline unions springing up at that time.

Not only was each sister in the Roman Union to have a new sense of identity, she also had a new appearance to reinforce this. This all female group managed to reach agreement on that most personal of all things, dress. The new habit became a Roman Union hallmark for the next 66 years.

The Ursuline 'New Look'

Existing black habits were to continue for the time being but the finishing touches were a visual reminder of our internationality.

Paris- Cincture (belt)

Bordeaux- Veil

USA- Bandeau (headpiece)

Angers- Wimple (white chest piece)

Toulouse- Crucifix

Italy- Ring

Ursulines in England in 1921

The most striking thing shown in the map below is the number of French Convents in exile in England as a result of France's anti-clerical laws in 1904, which forbade any teaching of religion in school.

As you will see, several of these convents had already joined the Roman Union in 1900. After the initial traumas of resettlement, many of these thriving foundations established Novitiates and successful schools. These foundations became the backbone of the English Province which was established in 1923, with the Provincial House based at Crewe.

1 CREWE
Founded from Rouen in 1907

2 CHELTENHAM
Founded from Angers 1910

3 BIDEFORD
Founded from Avallon 1906

8 GREENWICH
Founded from Duderstadt Gravelines 1877/1892

7 FOREST GATE
Founded from Sittard 1862

6 THORNTON HEATH
Founded from Bordeaux 1912

5 WESTGATE
Founded from Boulogne 1905
Bideford 1926

4 BEACONSFIELD
Founded from Quimperle 1907

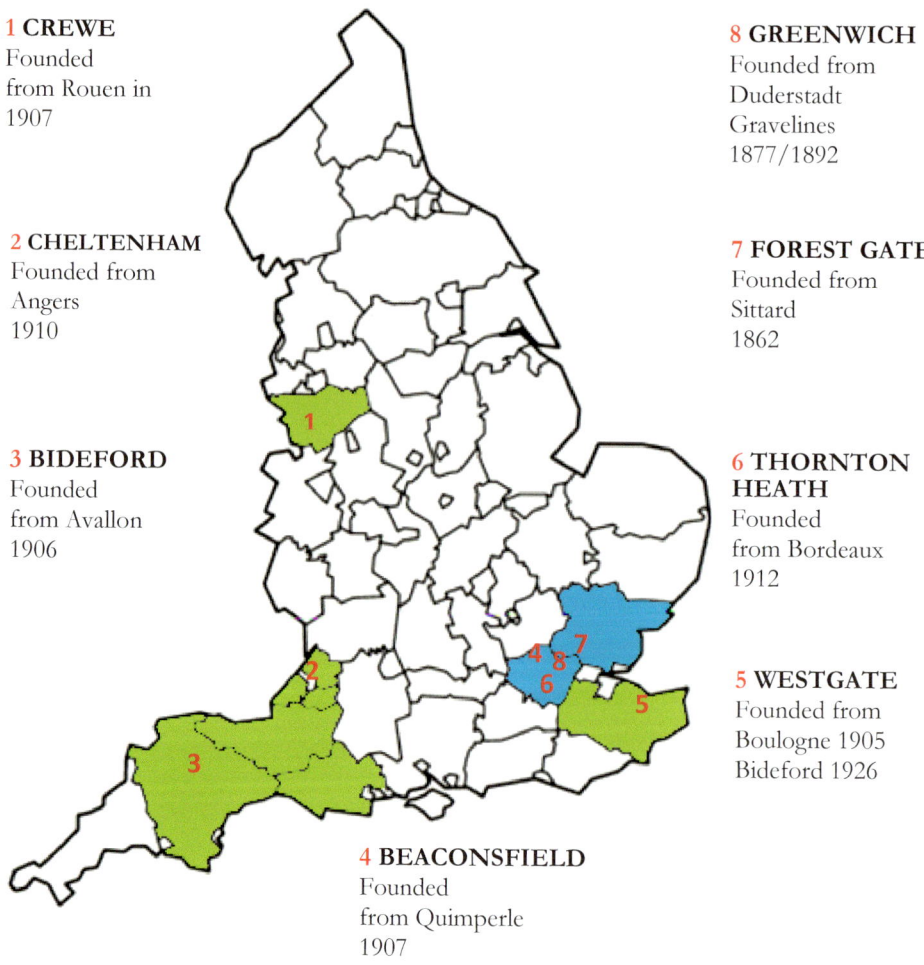

English Province Beginnings

The Story of Crewe

In 1907 the exiled convent from Rouen settled in Crewe, a very favourable choice since this town was a strategic railway hub. The sisters were fortunate to have a purpose built school and convent funded by families and friends of the exiled French sisters. This foundation was well run and quickly attracted a number of women from Ireland and the more Catholic North of England. It was forward looking and eager to promote the idea of an English province. Crewe itself joined the Union in 1918.

The convent bought land for development and sent several of its young nuns to Manchester University. In 1923, Crewe became the first Provincial House of the newly formed English Province and plans were made to set up a House of Studies in Oxford so that in June 1924, Crewe bought 66 Banbury Road, Oxford. There were high hopes the expense would be recouped by sisters from other provinces and congregations, using the house as an undergraduate hostel.

Unfortunately, subsequent developments did not favour Crewe. The French bishops were eager for exiled convents to resettle in France. Crewe was large and well established and seemed sound enough to support convents in both places, but the Rouen convent had been destroyed during this time of exile. Mère Cécile Luce, foundress of Crewe, was recalled to manage this resettlement. To do so she borrowed money from the Ursulines in the USA and repayment of this debt fell to Crewe, as the convent had been largely paid for by subscriptions from France.

Mère Cécile Luce

The Crewe convent had the opportunity of taking over the boarding school of Dee House and the Parish elementary school in Chester, at that time run by the Faithful Companions of Jesus. This they were happy to accept. Both still exist, Dee House has now been subsumed into St Bede's Catholic High School and the elementary school is now St Werburgh's Primary. Unfortunately, this was not the last of their financial commitments.

In 1927 Forest Gate, and other houses founded from it, joined the English province of the Roman Union; the thrust was now Southwards. It was considered best, therefore, for the House of Studies to be in London and the Novitiate and Provincialate to be in Westgate, Kent. Crewe was now faced with unsustainable debts; in 1933, it closed. A sad event which like many events in history is called into question even to this day.

Roman Union Membership 1923

The pictures below show the English houses that joined the Roman Union first in 1923. Crewe, Greenwich, Bideford, Beaconsfield and Dartford (no picture available).

CREWE PROVINCIALATE　　　　**BIDEFORD**

GREENWICH　　　　**BEACONSFIELD**

The Dartford Convent has a different history. It belonged to another religious family altogether and took the name Ursuline as it was virtually synonymous with Girls Convent Schools in France. These sisters too, were exiled to England because of anticlerical laws. They were a small group and found themselves alone in exile and in 1911, asked to join the Roman Union, which they did. They were affiliated to the Dutch province. In 1923 when the English Province began, they became part of its first five members. The following year, however, the convent was closed and the sisters went to various places. Bishop Amigo then asked the Ursulines to open a convent in Sevenoaks, Kent; this convent closed in 1927 and the sisters moved to Westgate.

The absence of the pre-existing English Houses Forest Gate, Brentwood, Billericay, Palmers Green and Wimbledon will not have gone unnoticed.

But if Crewe had some reservations about the possible outcomes of joining the Union, Forest Gate and Wimbledon were eager for links. Links that would recognise internationality and at the same time give scope for 'Englishness' and less dependence on local bishops. As early as 1872, Mother Victoire, superior, wrote to Cardinal Manning telling him how isolated the Community, then the only one in England, felt. She was asking permission to be affiliated to the Ursulines of Rome. Forest Gate's archives also recorded reservations about the appropriateness of the central novitiate in Haacht, Belgium for English novices, especially lay sisters.

Forest Gate *(right)* heard rumours of a general meeting in Rome at the invitation of the Superior of Blois. The rumour is mentioned in both the minutes of the local council and the archives of the house, both recording that no invitation was ever received at Forest Gate. Bishop Doubleday, Bishop of the newly created Diocese of Brentwood, when asked his advice said, "It seemed a good thing and he would have no objections". In 1908 Cardinal Bourne told the community "You must now consider for yourselves whether your motives for not joining the Roman union are sufficient to outweigh the Pope's undoubted desire for union".

Wimbledon too, by now an independent house, had the support of Archbishop Amigo of Southwark who advised the community to join the Union. He wrote, "Take the vote of the community mothers and if they are satisfactory I will not oppose you."

Why the Delay?

The real answer is no doubt multifaceted and mired in history, but one factor undoubtedly was a sense of loyalty to their Belgium founder and foundresses who were from Tildonk, now part of the flourishing Congregation of Tildonk to which many English Ursuline Houses already belonged.

Cardinal Gossens of Belgium, a strong supporter of the sisters, directed the Mother General to say, "It was his wish that the Congregation of Tildonk should take no part in the movement for the moment." Forest Gate's response was "We would act with Tildonk as one body."

But...

By now an English Province had been established with a novitiate at Crewe. Forest Gate had a new superior, Mother Bernard Flood, who could wait no longer. In September 1926, supported by the Superiors of Wimbledon and Palmers Green, she wrote to Mother St Joseph Ryan, the Sister in charge of the Province (Provincial) at Crewe, proposing these three communities should join the Roman Union.

Mother St Joseph visited each of the three communities accompanied by sisters from Crewe, so that each community was fully aware of what they were undertaking. Each community took a vote. A positive decision was reached all round and on the 6th December 1926, a formal application from all three communities was posted to Rome.

On 18th January 1927, Forest Gate, Palmers Green and Wimbledon became members of the Roman Union, English Province.

"Have hope and firm faith in God, for he will help you in everything"
St Angela Merici

Ursuline Missionary Influence

Our Missionaries

Sister Mary of the Incarnation

In 1639, Mary of the Incarnation embarked for Canada, in order to found a house for Jesus and Mary among the indigenous people and to educate the French and native girls in Quebec. Since then many Ursulines the world over have been influenced by her call.

As has been seen from early days, there was a very rapid expansion of Ursuline Convents in Europe and by the 20th Century, this was worldwide, so awareness of the Missions was in our genes.

Ursuline sisters exiled from Germany settled in Greenwich in 1877. Not long afterwards Bishop Elzear Torregiani of New South Wales, who had known the Ursulines when he was superior of the Franciscan Capuchins at Peckham, wrote begging for a foundation in Armidale to help establish Catholic education in his young diocese. Ten members of this exiled community volunteered to go to Australia.

The travellers left Greenwich on the 24th May 1882, the Feast day of Our Lady Help of Christians, the Patroness of Australia, and embarked on The Duchess of Edinburgh *(right)*, having declined an offer of a first class passage on a faster boat. Providence was guiding them, for this ship was lost at sea with all on board. Their voyage lasted three months and The Duchess of Edinburgh docked safely in Sydney harbour on 28th August 1882.

Bishop Torregiani escorted the Ursulines to Armidale *(left)*, which they reached on the 11th September; handing over the residence he had prepared for them saying "This house belongs to you and your Ursuline sisters and no one, not even Bismarck can take it from you!"

Roman Union Response
THE ENGLISH PROVINCE, CARIBBEAN AND SOUTH AFRICA

From the Roman Union's first beginnings successive Mother Generals have ensured that all communities were aware of the existence of each other, especially developing missionary communities. Mother General, Mère St Jean Martin was profoundly moved by this missionary call and wrote how she hoped to establish the administrative organisation of our missions by connecting each one with either a European or American Province. Each of these provinces would be called upon to provide sisters for the mission, which had been entrusted to it. When Mother Dominic Tizzard learnt that the missions of South Africa and Guyana had been entrusted to the English Province, she wrote to Georgetown saying "We are sending you our best."

Mother Angela Woods turned out to be one of our very best. She was born in Brentwood, Essex to a large family. Her education began at home with her mother. She often spoke of the excellence and thoroughness of her upbringing and there was nothing like 'good home training'. The family eventually left Brentwood and moved to Wimbledon for the sake of the children's education. The boys went to the Jesuit College and the girls to the Ursuline Convent as day pupils.

At the age of 21 she joined the Order, making her postulantship at Wimbledon where she was kept a longer time than usual to continue her studies. She spent the first year of her novitiate in Belgium and returned to Wimbledon to complete her novitiate and take her vows, which she did on 2nd February 1906. After many years of excellent work in the school, she was elected Prioress of Wimbledon and held that position for six years.

When the Ursulines joined the Roman Union, it was decided that the Novitiate would move from Crewe to Westgate. Mother Angela was appointed Mistress of Novices in 1929 and expected to remain so for some time. However, she accepted the unexpected challenge to be a missionary and on 27th August 1931, arrived in Barbados as Prioress. Two years later, she became Superior of the Missions of British Guiana and Barbados and a key figure in the development of its mission.

Although her duties as Superior of the Mission and Prioress of Georgetown were heavy, she took her share of the day's work in the classroom. She dedicated herself to the children and their education. No one was too insignificant to come under her notice- if she had a preference it was for the poorer and more destitute. She was not into preaching but her actions and devotion to duty spoke more strongly than any sermon could have done. She lived first what she expected her children to be.

Mother Angela was able to visit Wimbledon once more, in April 1938, on her way back to the mission after the General Chapter in Rome. The house diary of the convent records how "it seemed like a dream to see her sitting there at the table while she told us all about the Barbados convent and the conditions under which the mission is carried on. The work is very hard as their numbers are so few, and they are greatly in need of help, financial and other." She also talked to the school children at Wimbledon about the mission and her newsletters were eagerly awaited and published in the school magazine. She died on the mission in 1945.

Missionary Visitors

As we shall see later, our schools were kept well aware of both missions by frequent letter contact and visits from sisters on route to General Chapters, and Tertians, returning from their year's renewal in Rome. They became well known to our communities, particularly the Guyanese, as they came for professional training and in some cases Novitiate.

Until 1966, when Guyana received its independence, teachers serving there required British qualifications. Before World War II broke out it was customary for sisters to come to England for training. This was resumed after the war and many of us came to know our contemporaries well as we shared our religious lives, our studies and the developments in a church on the brink of Vatican II. Guyanese Sisters discovered snow and that it was possible for the sun to shine brilliantly and still be freezing, while we discovered just how delicious Rum Cake was and how hot Pepper Sauce could be!

Several English Sisters went to both provinces as Missionaries, often returning for holidays or retirement. We would also meet up again for our Renewal year (Tertianship) in Rome. The church grew in these countries, as did a natural move for independence. Initially these regions were dependent on England and our Provincial was theirs, but in the 1953 Chapter, these Missions became independent and self-Governing. Mother Xavier Rowntree, a Missionary from England, became the first Provincial of what now became known as the Caribbean Province. During her time there the province came to include Venezuela and Jamaica, so the Caribbean Province became international, covering four countries. In November 1955, South Africa also became independent with its own Provincial Clare O' Connell. In more recent times, Sisters Margaret Woodvine and Jeanette Essey have always cherished the links we have had with both these regions and they are 'close relatives' in our Ursuline family. It has become increasingly customary for Missionaries to return to the mother country for their retirement.

The early decades of the 20th century, particularly the period between the two World Wars, saw a great upsurge of missionary zeal throughout the Catholic Church. This was felt in parishes and also in schools where a special association was created to sponsor awareness in young people of overseas missions. It was called the 'Pontifical Association of the Holy Childhood'.

Ursuline Missionary League

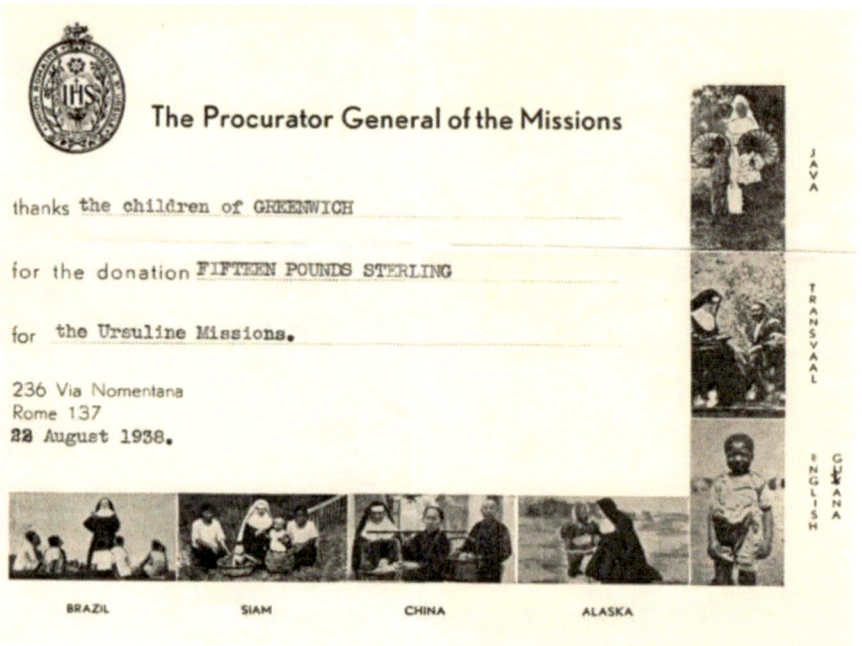

A Certificate of thanks to Greenwich Students From the Generalate in Rome, for their Mission Collection 1938

Mission awareness quickly became a feature of Ursuline schools, and in each school, a sister was appointed with the extraordinary title Zelatrix. Their task was to set up an Ursuline Missionary League (UML) to stimulate interest and knowledge in missions and to make this tangible in practical ways.

Most English Ursuline students can recall exciting stories from missionaries, for example, igloos in Alaska, bush schools in Africa, pictures of St Anne's orphanage in Georgetown and the many fundraising quizzes, raffles, as well as the Annual Missions Fair.

This tradition is still very much alive today, with staff and students taking a lively interest in the educational, geographical and economic developments of our specific missions and the many countries that are brought to our attention by world tragedies today increasingly, within our own borders.

Alaska Story
Sr Maureen Moloney

"While a student at St Angela's, I attended as many UML meetings as I could. The Sisters running the after school club worked very hard on preparing the content. This information gave us great inspiration and a wealth of knowledge of how people lived in different lands from ours. We were often given handouts about specific "missions" and a flyer on Alaska prompted me to get an Alaskan pen friend.

The Native American student I had was Angela Joseph from Andreafski. We corresponded for a long time but I rarely managed to read her letters first hand! My mother was so interested in them she opened and read them first, before I had arrived home from school!"

Philippines Payatas Dump Project

One long-running project supported by Ursulines in England, Ursuline schools, our Serviam association, other schools, parishes, families and individuals, began in 1999 and continued for over 10 years. This was the Philippine Payatas Dump Project. The work on site was masterminded by Sr Johana Mughira from the Indonesian Ursuline province. Sr Johana came to England in the summer of 2000. She visited the schools

and communities, to give first-hand information on how she and her co-workers could extend the work presently being done, to better the lives of the children and their mothers. This was advantageous in spurring the project on over the coming years, as the donors felt part of the project and owned it too.

The money was mainly used for giving livelihood skills to the mothers, working with the young children in a variety of ways, supporting individuals to go to school and to make sure those at the centre had a good meal each day. £45,500 was raised, mainly in the first few years, and the first of the projects was to build an extension to the centre. Sr Maureen Moloney worked at the centre for three months in 2000 and saw some of the projects as they began to blossom. Immediately prior to her arrival, there was a massive landslide within the dump and many were killed but also many were homeless, even from their shacks, and needed extra support.

One house on the dump site

Our Ursuline Missionaries

Sister Ellen Mary Mylod

She may be better known to some as Sister Mark or Nellie Mylod.

In 1944 she remembers, as an 11-year-old, I walked up The Downs to begin my first day as an Ursuline pupil in Wimbledon Ursuline Convent School. Uncomfortably clad in school uniform: hat (yes, we had to wear a hat!) with the Serviam badge firmly set in the middle, a blazer with the Serviam badge on the pocket and some cash to buy exercise books from the stationery cupboard, with the Serviam badge clearly printed on their cover.

In 1951, I entered our Institute. I taught at Wimbledon, Ilford and Forest Gate where I was Headteacher from 1966 to 1971. In 1972, I heard Sr. Teresa Lin, Group Superior in Taiwan, make an impassioned request for an English speaking Ursuline to come to teach in the Wenzao Ursuline College of Modern Languages in Kaohsiung, Taiwan and I felt drawn to respond.

I came here in 1973 on two-years' international service and faced unexpected adaptations! I had two classes of 50 plus, 17-18 year-olds, each for 18 hours a week and had to become fluent in Chinese!

I requested a third year of transfer to have time to re-inforce what I had begun. In the meantime, Taiwan was forging ahead, especially in education. To leave Wenzao now demanded discernment, which I sought. Result: a transfer without limit of time.

I'M STILL HERE!

On the 18th September 2021,

Sr Ellen Mary Mylod in the presence of the Mayor of Kaohsiung City, the Archbishop, teachers and many alumni was awarded

The Citizenship of Taiwan, Republic of China

She is the first foreigner to receive this award in Kaohsiung

CAMEROON
Sister Jayne Horswill (centre)

From its beginning in 1984, the community of Nagaoundere has been international, interprovincial and thanks to the Canadian Ursuline Union, inter-congregational.

The call to Cameroon was from the well-established diocese of Ngaoundere to work alongside the teachers and administrators of the College de Mazenod.

Cameroonian vocations gradually increased and so horizons widened. First of all, in a country of 230, not always peaceful ethnic groups, achieving unity in a community so diverse was a witness in itself. The community of Ngaoundere is now involved in a flourishing primary school, the École Ste Angele, in the parish, in social work for women and families and also in help for prisoners. Healthcare is of great importance for the surrounding villages of Ngaoundere and Sister Asta trained as a nurse and is now Director of the Diocesan Dispensary.

CARIBBEAN
Sister Katharine Glencross

As a child, hearing about the missionary work of the Ursuline Nuns, in the Caribbean, I wanted to go abroad and work with the children there. The Orphanage in Guyana attracted me, especially as in school we collected useful items to send to them.

My hopes were fulfilled many years later, when my request was granted and I went first to Barbados and later to Venezuela visiting both Guyana and Jamaica during my 17 years in the Province. My first two years were spent teaching in St Patrick's Mission school in Barbados. I began by volunteering, doing different things such as teaching the secondary pupils to read and assisting teachers. In Venezuela I taught primary students English as a foreign language and when I returned to Barbados after six years I had my own primary class. On Saturdays I worked as a catechist in the parish, preparing for confirmation. Looking back on those years, I am very grateful for all the opportunities that came my way both with the people I met as well as the beauties of creation.

English Missionaries

Rev Mother Joseph Ryan
Sr Ignatius Fitzgerald
Sr Ignatius O'Flynn
Sr Campion Gibson
Sr Xavier Rowntree
Sr Baptist O'Halloran
Sr Ursula Woods
Mother Angela Woods
Sr Katharine Glencross
Sr Jayne Horswill
Sr Gemma Bashford
Sr Rosemary Chambers
Sr Mary Carmel Pearce
Sr Mark Mylod
Sr Timothy Pinner
Sr Veronica Lyden
Sr Joseph Rowntree
Sr Anselm Peace
Sr Margaret Mary Hudson
Sr Martha Gregson
Sr Werburgh Bergin
Sr Gemma Feeney
Sr John Stahl
Sr Stella Smith
Sr Ursula Graham

Sr Maureen Coyne
Sr Dorothea Dawson
Sr Bernadette Rennison
Sr Aloysius Delaney
Sr Gabrielle O'Brien
Mother Michael Edgar
Sr Francis Needler
Mother Alphonsus Woodward
Mother of the Sacred Heart Dalton
Mother Assunta Ironside
Mother Scholastica England
Mother Patrick Harrington
Mother Stanislaus Munden
Mother Alban Holmes
Sr Paul Vidler
Sr Hugh Creighton
Sr Veronica Philips
Sr Magdalen Cleary
Sr Boniface Sack
Mother Aquinas Langridge
Sr Teresa Vaughan
Mother John Berchmans Hogan
Sr Ignatius Fernandez
Sr Gregory Hannon
Sr Ursula Wilkie

Firmly Rooted

1923-1966

Most dates have fluffy edges and this one is no exception. It has been chosen as it marks the beginning of the Roman Union in England and Vatican II (1962) which seemed a reasonable place to start.

In mid-19th century England, there was virtually no structured education available for women. Girls, it would appear, were incapable of assimilating serious education. The schools inquiry commission in 1868 complained about the poor quality of female education lamenting "the want of thoroughness and a system, the slovenliness and showy superficiality, the inattention to rudiments and the undue time given to accomplishments".

Strangely enough, the situation for English Catholic girls who had long been deprived of education was much brighter. The reason being that the Catholic Hierarchy was eager to re-establish Catholic influence in the country and education was its starting ground. Cardinal Wiseman looked to the continent where convent led girls' education was particularly strong. By 1850 over 50 different congregations had settled here and were offering education at every social level. These schools were run by several different congregations of sisters, who saw their work as a vocation, were well educated and keen to make a success of their new ventures

The Ursulines of 1862 came from Belgium as missionaries, eager to rebuild the Catholic faith, which had been driven underground for centuries. By the twentieth century two other groups, one from Germany and several others from France, both exiled through anti-clerical laws, settled in England and opened vibrant schools. At that time there were over 300 Ursulines in the country.

These sisters had been educating girls for three centuries. The sisters were consecrated to God, led a life of prayer and were committed to their work. They were also well acquainted with the educational needs of young women. Education Geography, "the use of Globes", Botany, Writing, Arithmetic and all kinds of Needlework! in faith was their primary goal, but they were also aware that pupils lived in a world they influenced, and by which they were influenced. Early curricula included History .

Education was by no means confined to the classroom. As early as 1898 Wimbledon archives record that a group from the school were "chaperoned to the Lyceum Theatre to see Ellen Terry (right) in 'Merchant of Venice'. They could talk of nothing else for days after."

The Board of Education was aware of the strength of Convent education throughout the country which is shown in their report from 1936 - "the considerable contribution to the education of English girls, apart from their religious and moral training, an education which embraces the whole person, the training of mind and will, the thorough and selfless care which girls receive…they need not fear comparison with secular schools."

Our Roman Union Ursuline schools, grateful as they were for their European roots, were also anxious to be integrated into an English world, with English ways. A very early Provincial Chapter requests that documents from Rome should be translated into English. So our schools began to embrace Englishness whole heartedly. One way of doing so was by pupils taking public examinations. This meant the schools had to be open to inspections, which also served to keep them in the public eye and to ensure teachers were professionally trained.

In the early 20th Century, Pitman's was among these examining bodies and England was a growing commercial centre. Suddenly a new, almost exclusively female career emerged and many of our schools developed secretarial sixth forms alongside the traditional academic one. These remained very popular with employers and students, right up to the days when we all abandoned our fountain pens in favour of tablets.

They were also helped by the Association of Convent Schools. An early professional association of congregations that shared the same apostolic zeal and were prepared to share good practice, problems and experiences. This was a vital part of Ursuline life and indeed of convent education throughout the country. Founded in 1928, it offered professional advice, ran annual conferences, summer schools and provided lasting friendships and camaraderie between congregations.

The English Province too had its own annual educational conference through which they could share good practice and get to know their sister schools.

The Foundation of Ilford

In 1903, Mother Regis Woodlock and Mother Cecilia Cremonini went from Forest Gate to Ilford at the request of Fr Palmer *(right)* to establish what is now the Ilford Ursuline Academy. For forty years the sisters travelled daily to and from Ilford to teach at the school. In September 1942 it was suggested that they live in a house near to the school, to avoid dangerous travel during the war. In November 1942, 6 Coventry Road was purchased and a small convent was established. In May 1943, the community of twelve moved into their new home and the following day, their friend Canon Palmer celebrated the first Mass for this community.

Ilford remained dependent on Forest Gate for the next year but in 1944 it became independent with Mother Joseph Powell as Prioress. She was also Headteacher and masterminded the transfer of a private convent school to a Government Direct Grant one. Under this scheme, 25% of Grammar school places were funded directly from Whitehall, with a further negotiable number provided by the Local Education Authority (LEA). Ilford was at that time part of Essex, so this involved working with an LEA in faraway Chelmsford, the Board of Education and individual parents of fee-paying students. She also had to cope with significant war damage repairs, which were not completed until 1948.

The school needed additional space, but Ursuline High School Ilford, bordered by roads on all four sides, had a very constricted site. This difficult phase of development fell to Mother Eugene Ryan, Headteacher from 1951 to 1967. Among other developments she was responsible for the gym and dining hall building, very "Avant Garde" in those days before the arrival of the Sports Hall/Dance Studios. She is also remembered for her "presence" and her gifted sense of colour, reflected in classroom décor and the beautiful pictures throughout the school.

Sue Riley, a longstanding teacher at Ilford shares her memories with us.

"Sister Eugene Ryan, or Mother Eugene, as I knew her, – and she was a mother to me from the time when I arrived for my interview, my first ever interview, with hat and gloves, shy, nervous and lacking in confidence - was the person who, after what seemed an almost casual chat, saw in me someone she would start on a path to happy teaching for 33 years at the Ilford Ursuline.

A formidable person in many ways, she was loved and respected by staff and pupils alike. I was very much in awe of her and almost trembled when she sent for me after my first two weeks of teaching - but it was to tell me that I was doing well! It was very comforting to know that she was supporting me from afar.

Very often, at the start of the school day, she would be in the staffroom, listening to our chatter, joining in occasionally, but mostly observing and offering encouragement when needed. This was how she got to know her staff and indeed how she came to know her pupils.

Sr Eugene Ryan

I learned many things from her. Seeing how she dealt with 'naughty' pupils taught me forgiveness and a sense of humour. I had a feeling that she was once a naughty girl herself. Another very valuable lesson for me involved learning how to ring the hand-bell in a hall full of chattering girls to bring about silence. All that was necessary was a single flick of the wrist – not a frantic shaking. The trick was to assume that there would be silence. This was a valuable lesson for a young teacher to learn, not just in ringing the bell but in everyday relationships with pupils - to assume that you would be obeyed, however nervous you were. This was very much an act for me at first, but it stood me in good stead as far as discipline was concerned.

Almost imperceptibly, Mother Eugene taught us that teaching is a very demanding profession, not just mentally and physically, but also spiritually and emotionally. I was relieved to know, on the first day of my second term of teaching, that she too had 'a nervous stomach' at the beginning of each term. As for the spiritual dimension, I felt very comforted to know that we had her support and the support of all the Sisters. I was happy to be able to practise and deepen my faith and to make it evident to my pupils.

I feel very privileged to have had Mother Eugene as the Head teacher who would be there as I embarked on the realisation of my vocation to teach."

Ursuline Primary Education

Ursulines in England have largely been associated with secondary schools and preparatory schools. This was never a policy decision but came about in response to the needs of the time.

In fact the first recorded account of Ursuline education in Forest Gate is of two French speaking sisters Agatha Langdale and Victoire Van de Auivera knowing only a few words of English, very soon after their arrival set out to Sun Row, to see the lie of the Land. Within a month, they opened their first school in two cottages in Sun Row, now Green Street. By 1863 they managed to relocate and St Ursula's Elementary school was opened in the former stables on the convent grounds. In 1896, St Philomena's Higher Grade school was added; their pupils could stay for a post elementary year. The present thriving St Antony's Primary School in Forest Gate is a direct descendant of these varied developments. Sr Kathleen Colmer, whose vocational preference has always been for primary education, was head of St Antony's Junior school and then the primary school until her retirement from headship in 2009.

In Wimbledon the Ursulines bought a house in Queen's Road to open an Elementary school, but soon south Wimbledon became the area of population growth so the parish school, St Mary's, was set up through the Board of Education's Dual System. It was large enough to embrace mid-Wimbledon in its catchment. Many years later Sr Damien O'Mahony taught there for a time, as did Sr Dolores Caine.

In 1929 Forest Gate Ursulines built St Vincent's Elementary Parish School at Becontree. Sister Campion Gibson was the headteacher there until her retirement in 1946. Sr Aquinas Hunt also taught there but as St Angela's was an expanding multilateral school she was needed there.

As we have already seen, the newly arrived sisters at Chester took over St Werburgh's Elementary school; Sr Helen Newton remained Headteacher there until her retirement in 1957.

This seems an appropriate point to hear from a primary practitioner.

Sister Jackie Doherty

At Christ College in Liverpool as a postgraduate student I found myself with time on my hands and was able to follow many primary courses. These were the early years of Christ College and an exciting time in education. I had my eyes opened to the new maths, the fundamentals of art and music development, the joys of exploring history and geography. I also did my teaching practice alongside Sister Alison Marjoribanks at St Nicholas in the city centre of Liverpool. Sr Alison was one of the most creative teachers I have ever known. We spent weekends upholstering apple crates to furnish reading areas and making multiple visual aids. Her classroom was a kaleidoscope of experience. She had hamsters, gerbils and birds, all needing care from her pupils who were among the poorest in Liverpool.

After a couple of years at Greenwich teaching English, during which I added to my skills by also teaching domestic science and art. I was given the opportunity to teach again in Liverpool at a very large primary school in Huyton. Harold Wilson was our local MP. This was an amazing time both in education and for the Church. The Charismatic Movement was strong. Creativity was top of the agenda for all classes. I could once again upholster apple crates to make separate sections in the classroom. We had our pet corner. Scouts came frequently to the school looking for lads to join the Liverpool and Everton football teams. There was a large mixed and well-educated staff. One colleague taught me Greek in the lunch hour.

When we left Liverpool I moved to Westgate and took up a post in the local Catholic primary school. Of the eight staff five of us were past pupils of Westgate Ursuline convent. We joked that the school was about as Ursuline as you could get. We all ran our classroom discipline much as we ourselves had experienced. Again, creativity was a hallmark of the education provided. Although I was not teaching in an Ursuline school I had support from my community and also visited Wimbledon Prep. school for a few days when I was asked to teach the infant class.

After Tertianship I was asked to join Surrey Docks, a community in south London and I again taught infants. The most satisfying age to teach for me was Year One. I learnt so much from my young pupils. They stretched my understanding of education greatly. The population changed in the time I was there from Irish immigrants to mainly Nigerian and Ghanaians. These new immigrants valued education highly and had different backgrounds. I began to incorporate more African dance and stories, and to become aware of art from different perspectives. I was lucky to have been teaching in a free and lively period when education was less rigid.

Later I would train as a psychotherapist and after a good few years of practice went back to primary school service taking with me a small black poodle as a therapy dog. In my retirement I was able to bring together all my experience in a new kind of volunteering.

Bell, Book and Candle

The restoration of the Catholic Hierarchy in England meant a gradual return to the rich Catholic Liturgy and practices, which had been denied for over 300 years. Despite much lingering opposition, the Oxford movement, the restoration of so many religious men's orders and the emergence of many women's congregations meant this was a religious re-awakening.

In the late nineteenth and early twentieth century sodalities, confraternities and guilds mushroomed in parishes and schools. Educating the whole person has always been vital to Catholic education and feast days and rituals added welcome lightness to the inevitable chalk and talk diet. The image to the right shows the Corpus Christi procession of Westgate evacuees at Rushe Court. There were also Cribs, concerts,

Christmas carol singing and Mission Fair days which all helped girls to focus on the prayer and social teaching of the church.

As sisters moved from convent to convent and school to school, they were able to share good practice and experiences and for a number of years sodalities became a feature of our schools.

There was often a different one for each year, but the principal one was the Sodality of Our Lady for the senior girls. Forest Gate archives record that in 1864, Fr. Mc Quoin who enabled the sisters to finally settle in England presented *"the first framed, illuminated manuscript of those enrolled as Children of Mary on 25th March that year."* The signed register of those enrolled up to 1963 still exists. In most English Ursuline schools 25th March or 8th December became a memorable gala day.

Gradually, fashions and devotions changed and in the post war period religion became more outward looking. World War II officially ended on 8th May 1945, leaving in its wake in England two fears, the threat of atomic war and a fear of Communist rule.

Two Jesuit priests Fathers Basset and Blake set up the 'Cell Movement'. It produced its own monthly guide and was based on Communist cell practice and Catholic Gospel Enquiry method of "See Judge and Act" principles. It was introduced in Ursuline schools and many will remember it from "Put Christ back into Xmas campaigns' which produced live cribs in town halls and shop windows. It also encouraged post school house groups to develop and enabled members to change what was possible when people worked together. English Ursuline convents were strong supporters of the movement and hosted a very popular annual week's Leadership Course at Westgate, offering wonderful opportunities for like-minded young Catholics to share their faith and ideals. It gave rise to many long lasting friendships and catholic marriages.

Today's Ursuline Links puts into practice those same ideals of faith and social action.

"I assure you every grace you ask from God will infallibly be granted to you"
-St Angela Merici

Statues and Gardens

Wimbledon courtyard

An inspector in 1912 wrote of Wimbledon "You have made a beautiful home for your children here and I hope they value and appreciate it and are grateful to you all, a devoted set of women." Ursuline schools are known to the outside world for their outstanding education and although students are also aware of how fortunate they are to have attended an Ursuline school; their memories are not only of the education they received. They also remember with great fondness their school grounds. Every Ursuline school has its own unique feel and the grounds contribute to that individuality

More recently a past student wrote "since I left, I've done courses in many places and I realise now how much the nuns cared for the fabric of the school and the environment in which we spent our school day." A sentiment no doubt shared by many who remember highly polished floors providing wonderful illicit slides, interesting classroom décor and beautiful gardens. It seemed appropriate here to revisit some familiar Convent/School gardens

Stained glass window from Ursuline High, Wimbledon

Greenwich front courtyard

St Ursula's Greenwich is positioned at the top of Crooms Hill and is surrounded by beautiful gardens and views across the River Thames. Students can often see boats making their way up the river.

The gardens are large and sweeping on different levels, laid to lawn with plenty of places to sit and appreciate the surroundings, particularly in the summer.

The church of Our Ladye Star of the Sea sits almost in the grounds of the school, acting always as a reminder of the close relationship between school, faith and the local parish.

Statues can be found throughout the school and gardens, the most striking of them all are the statues at the front entrance. St Ursula's sits high in the school frontage, with the Sacred Heart in the centre of the quad. Both of these statues are iconic for staff and student alike.

View of the church from the grounds of St Ursula's, Greenwich

*Stained glass window
The Ursuline Academy Ilford*

TULIP TREE LAWN

This impressive tree was already well grown when the sisters first arrived and is now well over 200 years old.

It is listed with Kew Gardens and tradition has it that there were only eight in England at the time.

Today it is a much loved feature of the school.

*Flower Garden and
Statue of St Angela
Ursuline College
Westgate*

1944 Education Act and All that

THE 1944 BUTLER ACT
PRIMARY SCHOOLS FOR 5 –11 YEAR OLDS
A TRIPARATE SECONDARY SYSTEM FOR 11 TO 15 OR 16+
GRAMMAR, TECHNICAL AND SECONDARY MODERN.

Selection for these groups was by an 11 plus examination

This image may look dramatic, but from the Restoration of the Hierarchy in 1850 the Church in England viewed education as vital to the formation and development of the whole person. From the beginning, it put the setting up of Catholic schools for the Catholic community ahead of building churches.

This civic involvement of the English Bishops in 1944 transformed the face of English Catholic education and the life of Catholics in England for all time.

Post war conditions were certainly opportune. The government was aware of the contribution differing denominations were already making to education. They also knew that with the many calls on their post war purse, they could not afford to ignore this provision. They realised it would require substantial government aid if the voluntary sector was to underpin the new Education Act.

The solution was a partnership agreed with government and voluntary bodies acting together to make "Roof Over Heads" provision by including

VOLUNTARY AIDED AND VOLUNTARY CONTROLLED SCHOOLS

The Catholic Hierarchy welcomed these new opportunities which allowed parishes and dioceses to provide Catholic education free at all levels to parents while allowing schools to retain the right to:
- appoint staff
- determine curriculum
- select pupils
- retain ownership of buildings

BUT

There was of course another side to the coin!

Schools came under Local Education Authorities and while salaries, books, running costs and internal décor were provided by the Government, the owners were expected to pay 50% of new buildings and external repairs.

The new act had a profound effect on the post war Catholic populace.

Ursuline Reaction

Sr Mary Angela Boord

Sr Angela Mary Reidy

From first arriving in the country the Ursulines had wanted to be part of the local scene offering an education that was at least commensurate with their local peers. They were therefore fearless and opened themselves to national targets, registering pupils for public examinations and presenting their teachers for public accreditation. They also sought out whatever scholarships, free places and special places were available to Catholics, through the government or Local Education Authorities.

Now they were anxious to embrace the broader opportunities available to Catholics through the 1944 Education Act and were strategically well placed to do so. Sister Mary Angela Boord was an enthusiastic educationalist, who at the time was responsible for Ursuline Education in England. Simultaneously, an Augustinian priest Fr George Beck with an educational background, was appointed auxiliary bishop in Brentwood; the diocese in which the Ursuline Convent schools of Forest Gate, Brentwood and Ilford were situated. He was also spokesman on behalf of the Catholic Hierarchy in government negotiations for the new voluntary aided agreement in the Butler Education Act.

St Angela's Girls High School, Forest Gate, together with West Ham Grammar for Boys, a fee paying Roman Catholic school, today St Bonaventure's, both in Saint Antony's Parish, opened as voluntary aided schools in September 1945. This was a completely new venture but with a different twist. It was the first attempt at housing the three different levels of secondary education, grammar, technical, and secondary modern in the one school in the local authority of the county borough of West Ham, a dockland industrial borough in the East End of London.

This must have been a proud moment for the earliest headteachers of Saint Angela's. Lottie Hynes, a boarder at Saint Angela's in the early 1870s when the school numbered 50, joined the community as Mother Xavier Hynes. She soon became aware that Forest Gate was a rapidly developing suburban area and needed a different kind of school, a Grammar day school. In 1879 she laid the foundations of Saint Angela's beginning with a dozen day girls. In 1921, when she retired, the school had 700 pupils and had substantial premises.

She was followed as head teacher by Mother Angela Boord until 1935, who subsequently became well known to the Board of Education, as she determinedly forged her way through the intricacies of voluntary aided status.

Ursuline Convent Wimbledon
Their route to becoming voluntary aided is well documented and makes interesting reading.

In 1935, Mother Veronica Paddison discovered that local Catholic girls who won scholarships were not able to take them up in the convent, so a campaign was launched with Surrey LEA and four "*Special Place*" eleven year olds were admitted, paid for by the convent. The following year the school which already carried the Hallmark "Recognised as Efficient by The Board of Education" qualified through an additional inspection to accept scholarship girls from local Catholic schools. Of the 31 new pupils admitted that September, 11 had scholarships. The numbers continued to increase and by 1939 the school was a two-form entry and more than half were scholarship girls. It is therefore somewhat surprising that in 1945 after some reflection it was decided not to take up either the Voluntary Aided or Direct Grant options.

From its earliest days however, the Community had been fortunate in the people, often-prominent local Catholics, who understood their aims and needs and were able to give support, friendship, and sound advice. George Woodcock, sometime General Secretary of the Trade Union Congress whose daughter was a pupil in the school, was a highly valued friend of the Community and always most generous with his time and farsighted advice. They were similarly fortunate in their Governing body and on January 20th, 1947, Mr Chuter Ede, then Home Secretary in the Labour Government, asked to join it. He had been Parliamentary Secretary to the Minister of Education throughout the War, and, as a member of the Surrey County Council, he was deeply interested in local affairs. Soon, he was playing a very valuable part in helping move forward the plans of the school.

Some lingering local and parental concern about change of status persisted. At the 1948 Prize Giving Fr Sinnott S.J. parish priest, spoke forcibly - giving a clear account of the financial position and putting before the parent's alternatives: "either a regular subscription of £50 covenanted, or revert to a fee-paying school." On November 2nd, Mr Chuter Ede strongly advised plans for a three-form entry school which he rightly thought would be required by Catholic girls in the area. On December 9th, the annals record the good news that "The Ministry of Education directs that we should be accepted as a Voluntary Aided school". So in September 1949, the school opened as a three form, non-fee paying grammar school.

St Ursula's Convent School, Greenwich

As we shall see later, Greenwich was the most severely bomb damaged of all our convents. In September 1945 the nuns were struggling to return to even pre-war conditions. Disruption to normal schooling through bomb damage repair, continued for several years and the prize giving report of 1949 opens with "This year again the school has been under difficulties owing to war damage repairs, which have continued throughout the year…Nor can we say the end is yet in sight!"

Despite this, the sisters had applied for Voluntary Aided (VA) status in March of that year but by July they were still awaiting the result. There was a delay as the VA body wanted a three-form entry grammar school, which the school challenged, as St Ursula's present condition made a two form grammar school cramped enough. In the face of this vacuum apparently created by officialdom, it was unequivocally stated at the same Prizegiving "The school governors and the LCC, have agreed we should best serve the Catholic interests of the district if we reverted to a 2-form grammar school. From this September we will be a 2 FE grammar school under the title **St Ursula's Convent School."** What happened next is lost in history, but common sense seems to have prevailed. Before the end of 1949, Voluntary Status had been granted and the school gradually evolved to a three form entry.

Ursuline Convent Chester, and Ursuline High, Ilford.

Although there was no overall secondary education in the country there was a substantial number of grammar schools and many of these were provided by voluntary bodies. To meet the increased provision required by the 1944 act, the government needed to keep them on board. So Direct Grant schools funded directly from the government came into being. The terms for these schools were: 25% places were to be free for children in primary schools and a further 25% available to the LEA should they wish to use them. The remainder would be open to fee paying pupils, who should be of grammar school ability and qualify through an entrance exam. Our Ursuline schools at Chester and Ilford joined this scheme in 1945.

Our boarding school at Westgate and the preparatory schools at Ilford and Wimbledon by their nature were not eligible for either scheme.

"The more you are united, the more Jesus Christ will be in your midst"
-St Angela Merici

Money Matters

The 1944 Education Act was new ground for the entire country and a steep learning curve at every level for the Ursulines, not the least of these were financial.

Forest Gate
At the stroke of a pen the sisters had undertaken to double the size of St Angela's in the next 5 years and had agreed to pay 50% of the substantial new buildings required.

Merici building

At that time Roman Union Ursuline houses had autonomous funding, although each house was generous in lending to the other.

Forest Gate community had assurance of salaries for those who worked in the school, and it was very significant contributions from these that underpinned their leap of faith. But there was a sizable bank loan to be serviced, so fundraising became added to the normal teaching load. Raffles, Sales of Work, Vanishing donation schemes, Miles of Pennies, became familiar events. Parents were encouraged to contribute £1 per family annually or split the contribution into 3 terms or pay 6 pence per week. But with £5 as the average weekly wage for many families this was not easy.

By 1975 they finally reached solvency and could take heart from the difference this had made and continues to make to the education of Catholic girls in this part of London.

Wimbledon parents were generally from a different social milieu. At a Parents' meeting on March 16th, 1954, a Parents' Committee known as the Friends of the Ursuline Convent, (F.O.T.U.C.) was formed, the Chairman being Mr Donnelly, Headmaster of St Peter and St Paul's Primary School in Mitcham, and the Secretary, Mr Donelan. Their aim was to help the Ursuline Convent School, by providing legal, financial and professional advice and above all friendship. By 1957 when the extensive building project began they gave invaluable support to the school and worked tirelessly and most effectively to organise schemes and events, notably the Autumn Fairs and Parents' Dinner Dances.. So here the debt vanished much more quickly than at Forest Gate. This group did indeed become friends to the convent and were a vital part of the school for many years, until they were subsumed into a more formal and very effective PTA.

In June of 1957, a ceremony took place which is unlikely to have been forgotten by anyone who was present on that day. A box containing a booklet giving the names of the Community, Secular Staff, and children then in the school, together with a set of coins of 1957 and casket of medals of a great number of saints, was placed in the concrete foundations of the extensive new buildings then being laid; a cache awaiting discovery by archaeologists of the future.

Roman Union and Our Schools

SERVIAM: HISTORY OF THE BADGE

"It is the wish of our Reverend Mother that all pupils of secondary schools and colleges belonging to Ursulines of the Roman Union should wear the same badge. The pupils of the Ursulines schools all over the world will thus easily recognise one another and unity of heart and mind will thereby be increased."

The badge was designed by two Ursuline sisters and approved by the Reverend Mother who explained its meaning in a speech she made in the 1930's at Valenciennes when the badge was given to her pupils.

"My Dear Children…on this badge you will see a group of stars, symbols of the ideal; the Cross, symbol of the Catholic faith on which your ideal is founded and the motto which expresses this ideal, Serviam: I will serve. It is the language of honour and Christian devotion to duty…You will live up to it by serving God…serving the Church…You will live up to it by serving your country, your family, your neighbour, devoting yourselves gladly to the service of those around you, to the Catholic cause, to those who suffer…Keep this ideal, carry your banner high, be worthy to carry it. Henceforth, Ursuline pupils will recognise one another all over the world… (the badge) will help you live a noble and holy life…".

I wonder whether the Reverend Mother truly envisaged a badge as widely recognised as that of the Serviam badge and just how great a symbol it would become. The badge today connects Ursuline students worldwide and never fails to send a wave of excitement through the young people when they spot their badge, worn by other students from another school or another country. Excitement that they share the same motto 'I will serve', the same values and the same pride in their school history and traditions. The Reverend Mother tells her pupils that the badge will help them live a holy life - the motto 'Serviam' is one that students carry with them long after they have left education. It is a tradition and a value that is instilled in every student and one that they never forget. 'I am an Ursuline' is a saying that is not purely reserved for the religious sisters but something that present and past pupils are very proud to acknowledge of themselves.

It is well known that as an Ursuline alumni, it is possible to safely travel the globe. There is an Ursuline Convent on every continent and with the badge in hand, acting as your passport, your Ursuline family is always ready to greet you.

Sr Catherine Kelly shares a recent experience with us - "While visiting one of our sisters in hospital, I got talking to the daughter of the patient in the next bed. When she realised I was an Ursuline sister she became very excited, as she was a past pupil of our school in Ilford. She then told me of the wonderful experience she had had when on holiday in Chiang Mai, Thailand. She and a friend were watching a carnival procession pass by only to see a large Serviam badge being carried by a group of girls. She said, "I really felt that I belonged".

Examples of different Ursuline School badges

New Orleans   **Thailand**   **South Africa**

The "universal" Serviam badge varies slightly from county to country, each place convinced theirs is the authentic original. But all are instantly recognisable and often forms the next sentence of the conversation.

Inter School Unity

As we have seen in the 'Emerging Roman Union' in the 19th and 20th century there was a growing desire for greater unity and sharing of experience among Ursuline sisters, who were now in many countries. A practice had grown up of sharing circular letters. As early as September 1876 the writer in one of these urged - "We should leave the status quo to which isolation leads to a teaching vocation. Let us exchange ideas. It will enlighten and edify us and there will be less danger of getting into the fixed ways of teachers who have no outside contacts".

By 1927, the English Province was well established and movement between schools and convents became a reality offering wider horizons to both sisters and students. Soon sisters welcomed the wider opportunities and it became general policy for sisters to experience several different communities.

Students came to know about other Ursuline schools. The Serviam badge helped create a bonding. There was a ready supply of penfriends from other places and, for example, regular French exchanges, visits from missionaries and from sisters from faraway places. London schools met for matches; Westgate Boarding school and seaside, became a popular sixth form outing. In 1952 Sheila O'Hagan of Wimbledon was responsible for beginning the Ursuline Netball rally which continued well into the 1980s. The 1st teams of each school competed against each other. This was followed by a meal where they got to know each other; with girls from Westgate and Chester spending the weekend with families from the host school. The first rally was at Wimbledon and they were also the champions that year.

Interschool exchange continues to this day in varying forms, often with differing groups spending time in each other's schools. In the past 13 years the schools have also shared in local and international projects through Ursuline Links.

"I shall always be in your midst, helping your prayers"
-St Angela Merici

Past Pupils have their say

Elaine Schreyeck

A past pupil of Ilford whose lifespan is just short of a century shares her life story with us.

"In 1931 when I was seven I started at Ilford Prep. I had previously spent 3 years at a boarding school as my parents divorced and my mother, unusually for that time, had to go out to work.

We were all evacuated at the beginning of the war to Ipswich, from September to Christmas. Even though the Ursuline school didn't take boys, I was allowed to take my two young male cousins with me! The local postman and his wife took us in, they gave up their double bed and I shared it with my cousins who were 7 and 9.

The school then relocated to Devizes in Wiltshire where my friend and I stayed with the French master at the local school. Devizes was a military town, there were a lot of soldiers and on flag day all the girls would go out and throw flags at the soldiers. The nuns kept a very close eye on us there!

I liked all the nuns- Mother John, Mother Veronica, Mother Clotilde and of course Mother Eugene whom I adored. I got A+ in all my exams. There were about 500 students, a large number, plus the Kindergarten. We used to play rounders on the courtyard and sometimes we went to the park to play tennis. The mistresses were all lovely. I made some very good friends and I was very happy at school. We finished our education whilst evacuated and I left in 1940.

My mother asked me what I wanted to do when I left school. I said I wanted to work in the film business, she said I had to learn shorthand typing, bookkeeping and continue with my French! So I went to Pitman's College for a year and then wrote to all the film studios but it got me nowhere! But I needed a job, an agency in Piccadilly offered me secretarial work in Paramount, Soho. Whilst there I met a lovely lady who had worked with Michael Balcon, head of Ealing Studios! She suggested I write to him, telling him that I wanted to be a continuity girl. There weren't any continuity jobs but they offered me a job in their script department. I earned £3/ 2/6d per week! To get there I had to take a bus from Ilford Station to Liverpool Street, a train to Ealing Broadway and finally the No. 65 bus to Ealing Studios and I had to be there for 8am!

At Ealing studios, Basil Dearden one day said "would you like to be my secretary?" He knew I wanted to be a continuity girl and if his continuity girl needed help, I was allowed on the set and could see what she was up to. Today cameras do most of the work but then the continuity girl sat by the director and cued the actors if they forgot their lines, took note of where everything and everybody was, what they were wearing. No detail could be overlooked. Even the number of takes! Usually people wanted to be a film star but I had read about continuity girls and I thought that I would rather be behind the camera than in front of it.!

I travelled the world making films. I did six Bond films, working with actors like Audrey Hepburn and Elizabeth Taylor but it was hard work. Sometimes I would be away for weeks or even months, but God was good to me in my times of doubt. My favourite place was Mexico. We worked in the jungle on a film about an Archaeologist and I spent Christmas there, which was wonderful; very Catholic!
I also worked on "The Nun's Story". I was in Rome when this true story arrived and someone suggested we make a film of it. Peter Finch and Audrey Hepburn co-starred in it. We went to Belgium and on to the Congo where we met Dominican nuns looking after children with different diseases and then further south to a leper colony, run by a Baptist minister. It was very challenging, we saw people without hands and faces. We went to Rome to film the convent scenes. We had a lot of extras dressed as nuns, but we had actual nuns guiding us throughout.

I retired in 1986 but continued to travel the world and have new experiences. My Ursuline education gave me a lot, it gave me a good basis of how to behave in different situations. When I was on top of a mountain in Greece an actor asked me if I had gone to the Cheltenham Ladies College and I said - No, The Ursuline Convent Ilford!".

4 Past Generations, 4 Schools, 1 Family

Carmel Swords (Reynolds)

Cis Heenan St Angela's

Our family has been associated, indeed educated, by the Ursulines for four generations, starting with my mother Cis Heenan. She was born in 1902 and attended the Forest Gate Convent, travelling daily by train from Seven Kings and was there during the First World War.

In our turn, we three sisters were sent as boarders to Westgate, the Ursuline Convent school on the Kent coast which was evacuated during the Second World War to Rush Court, on the Berkshire - Oxfordshire borders. This proved to be a fine

*Angela. Patricia, Carmel
Setting off for Rush Court*

house in the countryside with the Thames bordering it on one side and a home farm which specialised in prize jersey cows on the other. Since our family lived close to the east end of London we spent several of the holidays at school away from the bombing and so we got to know the nuns out of the classroom setting. I remember cycling one day, aged eight into Wallingford with Mother Gabrielle, known by all as Gabsy and challenging her to a race, but she replied anyone could do that and the real skill was in winning a slow bike race. I swear she could sit on a stationary bike indefinitely whilst I would wobble and fall off within seconds. She was a remarkable teacher and her lessons were a joy as she regaled us with tales of her travels on the trans-Siberian railway. The bell would ring for the end of the lesson and we were left begging for more

Returning to Westgate after the war we exchanged a swim in the Thames for a dip in the sea, the sizes of the classes increased and we got to play netball, tennis and lacrosse.

When the time came for me to send my own children to school it was the Ursulines I chose for my girls starting with the school in Ilford and then at Wimbledon. Though I have fond memories of my time at school I wanted my own children to be educated locally and to grow up with school friends nearby. My daughters Madeleine, Gabrielle and Francesca Swords attended the Ursuline school in Ilford from 1969 until Easter 1977, when they transferred to the school in Wimbledon which they left finally in 1989. Madeleine's daughter Tilly Milburn went to the Ursuline High School in Wimbledon from 2011 till 2018.

My class on the lawn at Westgate 1948

More recent memories of Westgate

In 1956 when I was 12 my parents went to live in Papua New Guinea. I had previously been at school at Chester but was sent to Westgate on the recommendation of Mother Ailbe and Sr Paul Flood.

The excitement of going to boarding school for an avid reader of Enid Blyton meant that I didn't immediately recognise what it would mean to be so far away from my family. The memories of filling my trunk with three pairs of every item of clothing carefully marked with Cash's name tapes was brought alive again a few years ago when I read the first Harry Potter book.

Westgate school was very small, only 120 pupils from ages 4 to 18, both boarders and day girls. There were a few day boys aged under 8. Most of the staff were nuns. The headmistress was Mother Henry Pendlebury. She was tall and very dignified and I thought all-seeing!. Everyone knew everyone else. We played lacrosse and I don't think I ever got the hang of it. Chester was a grammar school and academically more advanced than Westgate with the result that I was well ahead in my studies and got a good foundation as I repeated many lessons.

There seemed to be many school traditions. We had set activities such as hare and hounds on the feast of St Ursula. Older girls laid a trail up to the roundabout at St Nicholas and we all had to follow it. We had a walk every Saturday afternoon. This was sometimes by the coast and sometimes across the fields of cabbages. When we were in the sixth form we were allowed out by ourselves. I remember feeling very sophisticated going to the Ice Cream Parlour near Birchington Station for a coffee. Those were innocent days!

The sixties saw the beginning of change as the school was staffed by younger, more recently educated nuns. There were many boarders from the Caribbean at that time. They came through the Ursuline Schools in Venezuela, Guyana and Barbados. This meant that we had a first-hand experience of the international Roman Union. At this time my parents had moved to Trinidad enabling me to meet some of my fellow boarders at home in the long holidays. Very few children went home more than once a year if they lived outside Europe. Travel was far less usual. Being a pupil at Westgate brought us into contact with girls from all over the world. The predominant nationalities changed with world events but friendships were forged across nations.

There was great encouragement to read widely. We would have reading lists to complete each term. The education I received was not as complex as today but it was one that encouraged curiosity about the world about us. The basics were well taught and I am grateful for the good start I received.

Sister Jackie Doherty

From Chester

When I look back to my school days, which I do frequently and with gratitude and fondness, I know that I came away with a belief in certain core values that my school reinforced in me. Fairness, an ability to look behind the surface of things to see what else might be going on, a willingness to withhold judgement until I had more evidence.

Those things came from home too, but our nuns, through a gentleness of spirit and leading by example, also instilled that in me every day. I can always remember Sister Ignatius staring at the ceiling of our form room and opening with, "Someone here might have...." done whatever. I'd be left wondering who and what and confidentiality was never broken. No one was ever shamed or embarrassed but the matter was dealt with and closed because the "perpetrator" could trust Sister not to deal harshly, but quietly and kindly. It was a lesson I certainly applied in my own teaching career and the upbringing of my daughter.

I tell friends and acquaintances about our nuns and school motto surprisingly often. "SERVIAM" has followed me through my life, even though I haven't always managed to live up to it, I have tried.

My career in teaching led me to working with older children who had emotional and behavioural difficulties. From there I became an advisory teacher for Gloucestershire and then qualified for OFSTED in my mid-thirties.

Always, I thanked my school and my parents for putting me on the path to confidence and willingness to "have a go."

I was quite shy but our nuns were strong women who sacrificed so much for their beliefs. Sometimes, that thought would slip into my head and give me that extra bit of backbone when I needed it! It didn't matter if it was as headmistress or someone cleaning the school corridor with a scrubbing brush, they were a sisterhood and there for Christ, each other and for us. That is still with me and I shall never let it go.

Helen Livesley-Jones

Memories of a Greenwich Scholarship

"I grew up in Victoria Way, Charlton and went to primary school at Our Lady of Grace. It backed onto the private primary school of the Assumption Convent. Despite seeing each other through a fence at playtime, we didn't meet the students from the other primary school until we went to church. Students from both schools were able to mix and socialise by going to Mass and different church events.

I was evacuated during the war and on my return to London I remember walking to Sheridan Grove to sit my exams and in 1945 I was offered a place at St Ursula's. St Ursula's was a private school and my headteacher from Our Lady of Grace, Mr Lacey organised for me to gain a scholarship and he took me up to the school for my first day. My brother Alan had also received a scholarship. My parents said that they could not have two scholarships, so my father decided I would accept mine and my brother would not. This was unusual for the time, a girl given opportunities in education before her brother.

I was placed in the M's and met Sheila Cronley, a girl from the Assumption Convent who I had known from Church. She was a welcome face and friend as I found it very hard to settle into school as a scholarship pupil. I was aware of how different I was. There was a certain level of snobbery among the other students, some girls rode their ponies to school, it was a completely different world to the one I had known!

I remember going to buy the material to make my uniform as we could not afford to buy the uniform straight from the shelf. Although there was snobbery among some students, there was never such an attitude from the sisters and staff at the school.

Summer 1947 bottom row, centre

We wore a hat that we had to wear on our journeys to and from school but I would often carry mine until I reached the bottom of Crooms Hill and then put it on. One day I left it too late and put it on at the church. Later that day I was summoned to the sixth formers who told me they had spotted me from the art block at the top of the building not wearing my hat and gave me lines. I didn't make the same mistake again!

I loved our cookery lessons, which we had in a separate house where we would stay all day, learning about house work and cookery. I excelled at art and was entered into a competition for the Sunday Pictorial, I had drawn an image of the Good Samaritan. At assembly I was getting ready to sneak out early to make sure my friends got a space on the tennis courts (I was small enough to crawl out). I had nearly reached the back of the hall on my hands and knees when Reverend Mother called my name and asked me to stand up. I was bracing myself to get a telling off in front of the school, but instead Reverend Mother asked the school to congratulate me on winning the Sunday Pictorial competition. I was happy I had won the competition, but more relieved to have not been caught!

The grounds were beautiful, I could walk in them for hours and sit in front of the grotto and pray. I was invited to join the nuns on retreat at the school, where we were allowed to walk the grounds and use the chapel. One morning while we were sat at the long table in the refectory, I put my fork into my fruit and the juice flew across the table and hit Reverend Mother in the eye. Of course, we were not allowed to talk but she broke the silence with her shock! Everybody sat trying not to laugh but she was very gracious about it.

The teachers and nuns always looked after me, particularly Mother Peter Buck, Mother Anthony Lawrence and Mother Mary Clare Horspool, who was particularly

gentle and caring. I also remember when my mother became ill and was unable to do the housework, I walked into my kitchen to see my maths teacher standing doing our family's washing. She had come to the house to check on us and saw my father struggling with it- a true demonstration of Serviam!".
Mrs Ruth Drayson (formerly Bowditch)

End Piece

As we have seen from their first arrival the sisters were anxious to be absorbed into the national education system. It seems very appropriate therefore to conclude this section which ends in 1962 with this letter from the Ministry of education which clearly shows a rapport still existed between the gurus of Whitehall and individual schools.

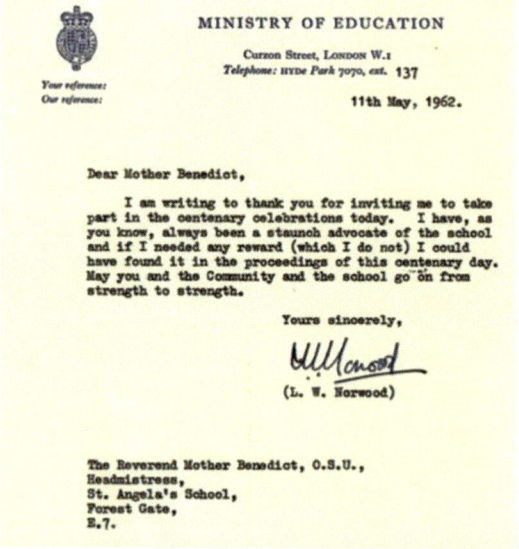

SR BENEDICT WITH UPPER VI 1962

Shaken to Our Roots

1962-2021

Aeons ago the psalmist wrote "Change and decay in all around I see." And for most of us old and young that is an indisputable experience but every so often there are seismic shifts and with hindsight we name them sea changes. Climate Change must be one such at the moment and the revolutionary spirit of the sixties seems an appropriate starting for this chapter. In England post war austerity was over, London became the centre of art, music and fashion. Universities were bulging. There was a sense of new life and hope. This movement of shattering change was also felt profoundly in the Catholic church.

The Sea Change That Was Vatican 2

On 28th of October 1958 Pope John the 23rd was elected pope. By January 1959 this "caretaker pope", who was 76 when elected, announced the second Vatican Council. Now 60+ years later it is difficult to imagine just how the announcement startled the world. As with all apparent change, its roots had been growing for some time. A post war and post 60's world was vastly different from that of the last Council nearly a hundred years earlier. The church aimed to acknowledge the profound changes humanity had experienced in the modern world and to relate to contemporary culture.

Initially the most evident changes for Catholics were in liturgy. Mass was now in English and Easter had its rich rediscovered liturgy. But throughout the four years of deliberation many other developments emerged.

Below are some quotations from the 16 Council documents.

It upheld
The right of parents to choose the type of education they want for their children, the importance of Catholic schools and defended freedom of inquiry in Catholic colleges and universities.
Gaudium et Spes
It said
The church must talk to atheists, a continual campaign must be waged for peace, nuclear war is unthinkable and aid to underdeveloped nations is urgent. **Gaudium et Spes**
It said
Marriage was not just for procreation and urged science to find an acceptable means of birth regulation.

Gaudium et Spes
It said
That religious liberty is a right founded on the dignity of each person and that no one should be forced to act in a way contrary to his or her own beliefs.
Dignitatis Humanae,
It said
The Catholic Church rejects nothing that is true and holy in non-Christian religions, called for an end to anti-Semitism and said any discrimination based on race, colour, religion or condition of life is foreign to the mind of Christ.
Nostra Aetate

Vatican 2 and Convent Life

The most familiar aspect of the changes is that of dress; and feet and hair becoming visible! But it was much more far reaching than that!

There was a special document "Perfectae Caritatis" directed at renewal in Religious life.
If it offers relatively little in terms of concrete proposals, it nonetheless excels at its primary purpose, which is to articulate the wellsprings of authentic renewal for religious. (Practical Theology Essays on going deeper as a Catholic)

There were, however, two very concrete proposals which were unequivocally clear. There would be only one class of Sisters in communities of women. Papal Cloister was to be maintained solely for nuns exclusively leading a contemplative life. Enclosure and the distinction between lay and choir sisters had long been areas of concern to all of us so these changes were very welcome.

We were encouraged to look at the "what" and the "why" of all that we did and to responsibly present a personal view point no matter how many eyebrows it raised. Special Constitutional Chapters were held in each Order where the emphasis moved from legislation to inspiration and "ad experimentum" was favoured over "decree." Constitutions became "user friendly." Ours became "Lead a New Life" and "Unity in Diversity"- our rallying call.

The transition from "THEN TO NOW" however was neither seamless nor painless, as we tried to agree how best to "return to our origins" and "adapt to the changing conditions of our times", but from today's viewpoint this was a road profitably and welcomely travelled.

As you will see in "Our Way of Life" Vatican II has shaped and continues to influence our Prayer, Community and Mission now and into the future.

What's in a name?

As already stated one definitive decree of Vatican II was that there would only be one class of sisters, so henceforth there would be no distinction between lay and choir sisters and there would only be one title of sister- 'Mother' would be redundant. Up to this point it was customary for sisters to take a specific saint's name; there was now an option to re adopt one's own Christian name. Several sisters did this after the 1968 general chapter, but there were also many who have done so at various stages since. There were also those who adjusted the spelling of their name, or adopted part of it. This will present some confusion to many readers, so the first time a changed name is used we will put the former one in brackets.

It is also evident that for many years, we have felt uncomfortable with two classes of sisters, but it would be a great disservice if we let this historical hiccup overshadow the vibrant contribution the lay sisters made to our lives and that of very many children. They had a different agenda and a different role. They were great homemakers and often provided real friendship, good fun and a different outlook. Most of us have favourites we keep alive in our memories. This is also true of many students.

"It didn't matter if it was as headmistress or someone cleaning the school corridor with a scrubbing brush, they were a sisterhood and there for Christ, each other and for us." **Helen Livesey-Jones, Chester past pupil**

"It was by no means only the teaching nuns who gave the school its character as a convent school. While the distinction still existed between Choir nuns and Sisters, those of the latter who cleaned the school and worked in the kitchen often became great friends of the girls during the dinner hour and at break times. The social life of the school was poorer when the Sisters were no longer involved in cooking and serving dinners, and the happy hours of chatting in the kitchen were a thing of the past." **The Ursuline Chronicle, Wimbledon.**

Many Westgate boarders far from home remember a sister's smile at homesickness times!

This seems an appropriate place to insert Sr Mary Ita's profile, beginning as it does with Barbara Layton's school memories.

Sister Mary Ita O'Riordan

"I was a pupil at St Angela's, Forest Gate 1952-1959 when school dinners were the norm, some days were better than others. I can't remember a day when Sr Mary Ita wasn't serving behind the dinner hatch, her lovely smile not only lit up her face but cheered us girls up waiting in a long and tedious queue.

Her voice was gentle and smiling and had a lovely Irish lilt. No matter what vegetable she was giving us, it came with happy and encouraging words! These were not the days of generally happy faces for nuns, teachers or the domestic sisters- so she stood out like a shining star in the middle of every day."

Four women came from Ireland, three from one family and one from another. Brendan, Mary Ita, Anne (who sadly died during her novitiate) and their cousin Kieran. They all had the same surname of O'Riordan and their arrival caused something of a stir. This was wartime and aroused spying concerns; an officer from a special police branch arrived at the Westgate convent to interview Sr. Kieran!

The "O Riordans." as individuals and a clan, made a significant contribution to Ursuline life.

Mary Ita held various roles in Greenwich, Forest Gate, Wimbledon, Westgate and Silvertown. She was a great storyteller and had a fund of jokes from the magazine 'Ireland's Own' which lost nothing in the telling. She was always very popular with school girls in the many places she served. She entered the convent young and easily established a rapport with others and was good company.

She is the last survivor of her family and at 94 is no longer able to tell her own story, but the most recent years are alive in most of our memories.

In 1989 we opened a small community in Silvertown Newham, East London. A new interfaith church was opening in Beckton and Sister Alison Marjoribanks was asked to be its coordinator. Mary Ita became one of the founding members of this new community. There she became a parish worker and a chaplain in Newham General hospital. Both proved to be roles in which she was eminently suited. The Parish priest once said "She could make a lamp post talk!." The Newham General Hospital so appreciated her work that she was asked to represent them at a Buckingham Palace Garden Party, where, Irish as she was, she was delighted to "meet the Queen!." She loved her time at Silvertown and if you go there you will bump into many people who still remember her with affection.

Our way of life

Although outwardly life seemed more relaxed, Vatican II was not intended to be an easy option or to lessen the depth of commitment. Through prayer, discussion, experiment and reflection we were challenged at our roots to Lead a New Life. and the call to **Prayer**, **Community** and **Ministry** remained our vibrant mission.

In this section we will reflect on the last 60 years of Roman Union Ursuline Life under three headings Prayer, Community, Mission .

P

Praying alone and together is woven into our day and strengthens our sense of mission.

R

At daily Mass and prayer in community we are united with the Prayer of the Church and our part within it.

A

In personal prayer we aim to deepen our closeness to Jesus, strengthen our faith and, in union with the whole church, make his presence more known in the world.

Y

E

People often ask us to pray for them, especially at times of sickness, trouble or celebration. Our prayer gives us an opportunity to pray specifically for these people, and so to bring them to the centre of our lives.

R

"God alone knows what you need and can and wants to provide for you."
-St Angela Merici

Prior to Vatican II the Liturgical life of the convent and parish ran on parallel lines. Local priests celebrated Mass and Benediction at both the convent and the parish. With enclosure restrictions now moved, many sisters began to feel a call to be more involved with parish communities, especially as the council called for greater lay involvement. Sister Jenny shares her experience as a full-time trained parish sister and Sister Dorothy, that of a retired teaching sister offering full time commitment to the Sacred Heart Parish Wimbledon.

Parish Ministry

Sister Jenefer Glencross

"I had not planned to take up parish ministry. It happened when the Provincial Sr. Ignatius, allowed me to take time off for a course, after a stint of teaching in our boarding school at Westgate. The Pastoral Ministry course at Dublin attracted me. My aim had always been to encourage the students to take an active role in their parishes. It seemed a good idea to discover more about the reality of parish life, especially the scope for lay involvement. By September 1983 I had enrolled for a Diploma in Pastoral Ministry at Dublin Institute of Higher Education and settled into a sprawling ramshackle Georgian building in Mount Joy Square Dublin 1.

During the holidays I was based at our community at Shotton, in North Wales. It was my first taste of a small parish community without a school apostolate. The Pastoral Ministry Course was concerned with implementing the vision of the Second Vatican Council of a Church where the laity played a full part. The hope was that a less hierarchical style of Church would bring new life and energy to the parish.

As the course progressed, I became committed to this aim and asked Sr. Frances Oakley, who was by then Provincial, if I could take up parish ministry. Sr. Frances assigned me to the Ilford community to work with Fr. Kieran Dodd in the parish of St. Peter and Paul. My task was to train lay catechists and with their help, to establish sacramental programmes in the parish. It was at this time that the preparation for Holy Communion and the Sacrament of Confirmation were moving from the school into the parish.

Then in 1989, while in Rome on Tertianship, I received news that I was joining the new foundation of Silvertown. Fr. John Armitage had requested the foundation, when he was appointed parish priest of the newly established parish of Silvertown and Beckton. We had a small house opposite the City Airport in the Royal Docks. Everyone in the community was involved in the parish: Sr. Alison Marjoribanks was appointed administrator of the newly built shared church and parish centre of St. Mark's at Beckton. Sr. Mary Ita acted as Assistant Chaplain to Newham General Hospital and I set up the sacramental programmes for the new parish.

I asked for a move to Wimbledon to be near my mother as she aged. I continued catechetical work at Brook Green near Hammersmith. Although the area was a great contrast to Silvertown, the work was the same. Pastoral Ministry has brought me into contact with a wonderful assortment of people, from East End rogues and West London gangsters to people of deep faith and devotion. It has been a privilege to share their lives."

Sister Dorothy Perrott (centre back)

"For many years I was under the impression that the role of Ursulines as educators in England was confined to schools or colleges and so for 35 years I was very happy and thoroughly enjoyed carrying out an apostolate in schools.

It was only since my retirement from the classroom that I discovered another dimension to education that opened a new world to me in the form of parish ministry. I see it as a development or growth rather than an alternative. The experience I gained during my years of teaching proved a solid foundation on which to build.

I have always enjoyed working with adults, both colleagues and parents and extended family members of pupils I taught. In the parish I have been enriched and challenged in up-dating and supporting parents of children being prepared for the sacraments in their knowledge and understanding of the Church and what it teaches. For so many the possibilities for their own faith development have been sparse and this form of catechesis is a great opportunity.

There are two particular areas that I find most rewarding: 'Landings' and R.C.I.A.

'Landings' offers a re-connection to the Church for those who, for any multitude of reasons, have lapsed from the practice of their faith and wish to re-engage. Through weekly group meetings, over a period of several weeks, there is time to explore where God has always been in their lives; to be in a safe place where past hurts can be healed, and where they may learn afresh the truth and reality of the Church and its teachings in today's world. Confidentiality, listening, prayer, and discussion are essential throughout, leading to a final reconciliation and celebration.

R.C.I.A. is formed of a group of adults wishing to learn more about the Catholic Church and feel drawn to exploring the possibility of their becoming full members. It's a shared journey of faith inviting participants to understand and experience the Catholic faith, individually and as part of the community. Some of those in the group will have been baptised in other Christian churches, some unbaptised but have an affiliation with a Christian community, others have a non-Christian faith and others come from no particular persuasion. My role is one of the team who journey alongside the participants, offer instruction and information about Jesus, the gospel and the teachings of the Church. We meet every Monday night and it's the highlight of my week; participants and the team alike learn and share along the way. It is truly a privileged, enriching and prayerful journey of faith leading us all to a fuller understanding of Christ and the Church."

Retreats

One important event in Ursuline life is our annual eight-day retreat. As a general rule, but by no means always, this took the form of a preached retreat to the whole community, based on the Exercises of Saint Ignatius and followed a regular pattern of talks, reflection and meditation. Retreats are valued by the sisters and looked forward to as a time of renewal, prayer and reflection. However, as with everything there are weaknesses. Their effectiveness depends greatly on the preacher, and one shape does not fit each one's personal relationship with God. There is also little scope for the feminine way of doing things.

This was of course well known before Vatican II and in the Juniorate we became guinea pigs for directed/ guided retreats. Once experienced, for most people these became a preferred norm. Annual retreats began to take differing forms generally, with participants taking a more active role; sisters too frequently chose to go to retreat centres, make private retreats, or retreats with a specific focus e.g.. art or music. For several years in the late eighties the province came together at Westgate for about 12 days. There each sister could choose one of four or five different kinds of retreat. Those who wished could then take part in a four-day conference on scripture, religious life or personal development, each with a keynote speaker. Many of our sisters developed skills in these fields, which they were able to share with other religious and laity.

Sister Felicity Young- Companions on the journey

"Blessed be the God and Father of our Lord Jesus Christ, a gentle Father and the God of all consolation, who comforts us in all our sorrows, so that we can offer others, in their sorrows, the consolation that we have received from God ourselves."

These verses from 2 Corinthians 1, verse 3, reflect my own experience as I listen to others in my role as spiritual accompanier/director. (The expression, "spiritual director" is an older term for one who listens to another concerning their spiritual life: it is a misnomer, as we recognise that the Holy Spirit is the director, and the accompanier simply listens with attentive reverence to the experience of the pilgrim, and from what they say, or sometimes don't say, helps them see more clearly where God is leading them.)

Like many Ursulines, I was a teacher, busy in the classroom, preparing lessons and correcting books! After early difficulties with teaching, I enjoyed the work, and I have always been interested in people, and liked working with them.

Over a period of time, I lost my bearings on the spiritual journey and needed help; at that time, spiritual accompaniment was not so readily available as it is now. My first experience of an individually guided retreat, where I spoke to the prayer guide each day, turned my ideas about God and myself upside down! The prayer guide was so compassionate and understanding, and helped me to grow in trust in God, and in good self-worth. Over the next few years, it seems I had many truly providential encounters with helpful people, just when I needed them. As the saying goes, when the pupil is ready, the teacher will appear. I received so much help from kind and skilful spiritual accompaniers, that I began, tentatively, to wonder whether I could help others in this way, "using the same help I had received from God" through others.

And so it was! The community was aware of the way I was thinking; and the very same week I was given permission to "look for a course." There was an advert in the Tablet for a spiritual accompaniment course in Chicago! God has taken me by surprise so many times!

This course was "tailor-made" for me. It was a holistic, creative course, involving every part of ourselves, body, heart, imagination, mind and spirit. We were encouraged to express ourselves through art, music, movement, poetry, story-telling, and dream work (this last was a revelation!) Participants came from many different countries and cultures, and I found it a deeply satisfying experience; it not only equipped me with listening and counselling skills, but more importantly, we were helped to work on our own lives, so we could become more truly ourselves, learning to be compassionate self-observers, and listeners to our bodies as an

instrument of discernment; through attentive listening to ourselves, we learn to listen well to others.

After the course, I had to learn patience! I discovered that if I tried to "advertise myself" nothing came of it! I had to wait for people to contact me, and gradually I found how one thing leads to another, and I got involved with a group of prayer guides in Kent, who invited me to be on a team organising Weeks of Accompanied Prayer in parish churches. These are week – long retreats in daily life, where we meet individuals each day of the retreat, listening to their thoughts and reflections; truly, God can work wonders in a week! This work led me to meet someone who ran a retreat house, so I was also involved in accompanying people making silent retreats. Gradually, people began to come for ongoing spiritual accompaniment at our house in Ilford, and now at Forest Gate. During Covid, my technical skills were stretched, so that I learned to accompany people online. There's always a new learning curve.

As I look back now over thirty years, I realise how blessed this ministry has been. I have listened to all kinds of people, of different races and social classes, various denominations, lay people, clergy (mainly Anglican) and sisters. It is an awesome privilege to be invited into a person's inner life, to hear of their struggles and joys, to witness how God leads each person on their own unique spiritual journey.

Back to our Roots

The council urged us to "**Go Back to our Roots**" and Sister Zela, conscious of St Angela's original foundation of a Secular Institute where women lived a consecrated life in their own homes, established a branch of **The Company of St Ursula** in Lancaster

Sister Zela Procter
Angela Merici: Vision Reborn 2009

On 25th November 1535 Angela Merici and 28 companions pledged themselves to a life of perpetual consecration under the patronage of St Ursula and her virgin companions. 474 years later, in Lancaster, two single women did the same.

This development grew out of a series of talks on different spiritualities given by Ursulines resident in the parish of St Thomas More, Lancaster. At the conclusion of the presentation on Angela's way of life, a parishioner said to me "I think that is for me." Independently, another parishioner had expressed an interest in Angela's way of life. We brought the two together and started a study of Angela's writings. This was the beginning of the Company of St Ursula, Lancaster.

In Angela's day such a step was revolutionary. The only life choices available for a single woman was a husband or strict enclosure in a religious house.

Our two initial enquiries made their first vows on 25th November 2009. This date marks the founding of The Company of St Ursula in Lancaster. Since then, four women have made their perpetual vows; a fifth temporary vows and a sixth has just made her first profession. They come from a variety of backgrounds and occupations, so from the beginning there has been growth.

During their two years of initial formations the candidates shared on the three documents of Angela. At the time it was the year of the consecrated life, so that provided more nourishment and hopefully they will continue to strengthen their consecrated life. From time to time they have retreat days. At the conclusion of their formation, first temporary vows are made for three years, followed by vows for life. Each month they have an afternoon with the directees with a contribution from a scripture scholar on a biblical book or text. The formation of each member is ongoing and she has to make a contribution both for herself and for others. They are financially responsible for themselves and remain in their current occupation.

Since the day of its formation the Company of St Ursula has established an international federation which is governed by a president and council which members vote to elect. Members can also take part in international pilgrimages and retreats. Any country or region that wishes to start a group has to apply to an existing group. The six members in England have made consecration for life.

Lay Participation

Sister Armida Veglio

Vatican II laid great emphasis on offering opportunities for lay participation. A proposal was accepted at the provincial chapter to form a lay association of lay people who wished to be involved in the spiritual and apostolic aspects of our life. At the time, we were also becoming more conscious of the obligation to promote the spirituality of the laity and their place in the Church; and of course, for Ursulines, to share the spirituality of St Angela and our own traditions with others. Below, Sr Armida speaks about her contribution and involvement in the foundation of Serviam.

SERVIAM

The idea of the Lay Association, Serviam, had been talked about for a long time. Some people had been involved with different Ursuline communities and were very interested. In particular it was a great desire of Vi Foss, a convert and friend of the Forest Gate Community, she had been helped in getting the necessary qualifications to train as a teacher by some of the sisters at Forest Gate and was keen to have some deeper collaboration. Her enthusiasm prompted some sisters to begin to explore how this could be realised.

In 1984 Serviam was formed as a private association open to all involving a commitment to daily prayer and the monthly meeting which included a talk and sharing, a meal and the Eucharist. Each community had a group varying in size from 4 or 5 to 20. A central committee organised the programme for each year and once a year there would be a meeting for all members. The groups had opportunities for pilgrimages to Desenzano and Brescia and to Taizé.

Many friendships were established and flourished among members and among members and sisters. The sisters were also grateful for the help and support that many members gave some of the communities. As communities became smaller it was difficult to maintain all the elements of the monthly meeting and so after a time it was the gathering together which was kept. Times have changed and many of the aspirations of the 1980s have been fulfilled. and the members of Serviam have gone on to contribute to society and the Church in many diverse ways.

The Serviam Promise

Almighty and eternal God
I wish to come closer to you
Through the life of prayer and to work for the building of your kingdom
In union with the order of St Ursula
I therefore dedicate myself to You as a member of
SERVIAM
And, with the help of our Lady and Saint Angela I promise to fulfil
the commitment of the Association.
Amen

Anne Richardson - Serviam member from Shotton

I was introduced to the Ursuline Community through my parish. I live in a small village and had a young family who were all in school. One of the Ursuline sisters, Sister Alison, offered to meet up with a group of mothers in our village to read and reflect on the following Sunday gospel with us. We met in each other's homes in turn each week. It made me realise how little I knew and understood and thought about my own journey in faith. I found I enjoyed these meetings; they made me prepare and focus on the Sunday readings so that on Sundays I was able to listen and be aware of the teachings of Jesus and not letting my mind wander so much.

The Ursuline community at Shotton offered the opportunity for me to join them and other like-minded people monthly, to pray and share my faith journey. I enjoyed these meetings and they gave me confidence. Other members joined from parish groups such as the ecumenical prayer group that met in the convent and from Cafod.

Serviam helped me to establish a discipline of prayer time each day and to think about God during the day. It helped me reflect on my day and look to see where I was handling things well and where I didn't do so well. It taught me to listen and watch and to concentrate on what was being said. It gave me support in prayer. The help and guidance of a personal prayer guide helped me greatly to expand my thinking. It gave me long lasting friendships. I began to read the psalms and scriptures and it was, and still is, like hearing them for the very first time.

I loved hearing about St Angela and have visited Lake Garda and Desenzano several times. Serviam taught me about St Angela's spirituality. It encouraged me to want to join in other prayer groups and to experience retreats led by the Ursuline community and other retreat houses. It led me to seek out courses that would encourage me and teach me about my faith and to help grow my faith. I was privileged to be able to volunteer in my parish and my local catholic primary school as a school governor.

The love and support from the Ursulines at Shotton also extended to my family and to the group's families. I am deeply thankful for all those who have walked with me throughout my life, who have loved me, taught me, supported me up to this time in my life. I am especially grateful to the teachings of St Angela's spirituality and for Serviam and the Ursuline Community for starting me on this journey. I can feel God walking with me.

> "I assure you that every grace you ask
> from God will infallibly be granted to you"
> -St Angela Merici

Sister Frances Browne

Frances could fit various categories here, teacher, retreat giver, counsellor, but in recent years she has been challenged by the completely different role of "long term sick" which has required specialised treatment outside our normal community structure. She is regularly visited by our sisters and greatly supported by Anne Griffiths who lives close by and visits daily. We are grateful for the support and friendship Anne is able to offer.

It is however important that we also capture France's (Sr Simon) contribution during her earlier years. Her first career was that of Home Economics teacher at Wimbledon and Ace Cook whenever it was needed. During her working life she taught at Wimbledon, Westgate and Forest Gate. She was great at her job and had very good student relationships. Later she was appointed Novice Directress and Prioress and later still, she trained in psychosynthesis and took up work as a counsellor and retreat giver.

She seemed to have a special knack of putting her finger on tricky situations and enabling things to change. I would just like to highlight two of these, which made a significant difference to two people's lives.

In the first case, a teenage girl had unexpectedly become an orphan and there was no readily appropriate solution. Unexpectedly Frances met a family who would be willing to foster, she negotiated with them and the outcome was very successful for both family and 'adoptee'.

The second case is completely different. Frances was working in an Essex Parish where she met a parishioner who had had a successful career as a secretary. She received a scholarship to St Angela's and treasured her experiences there. However grateful as she was she had never felt able to return, although past pupil meetings were common enough in her era. Frances met her in the parish and was able to talk through a problem, which had hung over for years!

She was an orphan, brought up, as many were at that time, in a Girls Children's Home. It was not a particularly bad one and she was well cared for, but it was institutional living and until she went to St Angela's all she had known. Initially she attended the local school with others from the home. They went en-bloc and returned en-bloc as soon as school ended.

When she and another girl qualified for St Angela's, academic work was no problem, but she became aware that other people led very different 'ordinary' lives. They went to each other's homes, shopped, made themselves cups of tea and played with brothers and sisters, when they wanted to. She also was aware that there was a certain veiled hostility at the Home, by both staff and girls at their new status, which made them 'special' and created 'Homework' which gave them certain exemption from chores.

They felt valued and treated as individuals at school. Frances managed to unravel her story and come to terms with the situation. She felt she wanted to pick up her school threads again which she was able to do. She came to a past pupils meeting and there met someone who immediately recognised her both from primary school and St Angela's, where they were both contemporaries. They were able to pick up their threads, share their lives experiences and discover that whatever the background school girls are apt to think everybody else's is more "with it" than theirs.

This woman has since died but was grateful for all the new avenues opened to her since meeting Frances.

"Act, move, believe, strive, hope, cry out to him with all your heart"
-St Angela Merici

COMMUNITY

We live our lives together; as far as possible praying together, eating together, relaxing together and sharing one another's interests and concerns.

Our shared life is a great source of strength; whatever our undertaking we know we are not alone but carry the support and good name of our sisters.

Our individual achievements are enhanced by theirs, and we are enriched by the prayers and attainments of those who went before us.

We try to make our communities places of hospitality, where friends and family feel at home, and where people who drop in feel at ease.

"Be bound to one another by bonds of charity esteeming each other, helping each other and bearing with each other."
St Angela Merici

Before Vatican II community life was shaped by two factors, papal enclosure and history. Papal enclosure could end with a stroke of a pen as it did in our 1968 Constitutions, but our solidly built schools and convents (usually on shared sites) that had become home to so many were another matter.

While schools remained our principal apostolate some sisters were experiencing calls to wider lay involvement. We were also all influenced by the changes available through labour saving devices and increased involvement with many people whose lifestyles were different from ours. The core ideas of a common life shared together and based on a genuine concern for each other remained, while we examined various ways in which this might be lived. So, community life came to be reviewed "ad Experimentum" Below we hear of our first development.

At a now enlarged Provincial Chapter, there was a groundswell urge to develop communities that were not attached to a school and be close to the poor in a more approachable building than our big convents.

Shotton

After due deliberation, we settled on Shotton in North Wales. The location was chosen because this once thriving steel producing town had become an area where practically all men and women of working age were unemployed as a result of a worldwide slump in demand for steel.

A community house was bought - no 2-4 Beaconsfield Rd. The sisters wanted to live alongside people who were actually experiencing poverty. They were to be self-supporting, so two of the sisters took teaching jobs in Richard Gwyn school in Flint, and one in the local FE College, while the remaining three explored their new environment.

They found they were warmly welcomed by the civic community and the local people and soon became well known and their house a drop in centre. There were two factors particularly in their favour. The much-loved Little Sisters of the Poor recently had to withdraw and had left a gap ready to be filled. Shotton was also an area of many differing churches, which had learned to work together for community wellbeing. The Ursulines became very much part of the town and ecumenical scene and enjoyed their life there until reluctantly we too had to withdraw after 35 years of Ministry.

The first Community at SHOTTON

Sisters
Josephine Baird
Phillip Rendall
Louis Marie Ryan
Teresita Clemo
Evelyn Mary Donelan

Sr Frances Oakley was responsible as provincial for stabilising our presence in the northwest of England when Chester closed and Shotton became a cluster community "Shotton, Lancaster, Wythenshawe".

Sister Frances Oakley - An Unusual Vocation

Her baptismal name was Shirley and she grew up in West Ham, East London. She was not born into a Catholic family but from her early life showed an interest in religion. She became involved in West Ham Central Mission, a nonconformist church which grew up in the beginning of the century, primarily to support the many people who were living in dire poverty in this dockland area.

When she was 11 she took up a scholarship place at Sarah Bonnell Grammar School which happened to be next door to Saint Angela's Ursuline Convent. She was always interested in science and when she finished her schooling she applied for a lab technician's job at Saint Angela's. It was to be her first brush with Catholicity. She was the first to hold the post. At that stage, teachers tended to be formal, gowned and elderly. Sister Benedict, headteacher, was not sure how comfortable the staffroom would be for a youthful looking 17-year-old starting something new. So, arrangements were made for her to join the Upper Sixth and share their cloakroom and break time. I (Una McCreesh) happened to be a sixth former at that time and it was my first acquaintance with Shirley.

At the end of the year I left school and Shirley continued for several years more as a Lab technician. She was naturally serviceable, made herself indispensable to the science staff and enjoyed her work. After some time she decided to train as a science teacher and went to Avery Hill training college, where she qualified as a teacher. She applied for a teaching post at Saint Angela's, which she had no difficulty in obtaining.

At St Angela's, Shirley decided to become a Catholic. On the staff, she met a History teacher of about her own age who had been a pupil at the Ursuline Convent Westgate. They became friends and both discovered they wanted to become nuns. So, she and (Sister) Zela joined the Novitiate at Westgate together.

After the novitiate, Shirley, now sister Frances de Sales, found herself once again teaching at Forest Gate. Science had always been her great love and at this stage Nuffield Science was making its mark and was particularly strong at Saint Angela's, because it was the special protégé of the LEA science inspector. On one occasion he was visiting the school and was nearly knocked over in the science corridor by one student pushing another on a trolley at great speed, only to discover this was an experiment arranged by Sr Frances and part of her lesson! I think he was secretly very impressed.

Frances did much to enhance and enliven the science teaching. The school became a member of the Wildlife Rangers Association. Frances and Sister Gemma with several other sisters commandeered from other departments, often took groups on

Wild Life ramble weeks during the summer holidays. She continued her science teaching at Westgate and Wimbledon, but then was called to the service of the Institute as Novice Mistress, Prioress and Provincial. It was as provincial that she was responsible for the development of the three cluster communities of Shotton, Wythenshawe, and Lancaster.

In retirement, she spent a Year in Skye pioneering parish work. It was probably there that she revived her accordion skills, which added a new dimension to community, social and liturgical events! She also spent two years in Billings working with Native Americans who were mainly victims of abuse; she held prayer sessions and discussions with them.

But it is mainly at Westgate where we chiefly remember her smiling and warm welcome!"

Sister Catherine Pennyfather

"The move to Stannard Court, a complex of retirement flats in Catford south east London began in 2008. Sr Anne Benyon had come across it. It was a new foundation and she introduced Sr Maureen Maloney, (the Provincial at the time) to it.

Anne was the first to move in, in September 2008 and she was followed by Sr Campion O'Hagan in October and I moved there in November. Stannard Court was very conveniently placed, the Catholic church was just minutes away and it was a wonderful parish which welcomed us. Anne and Campion both joined the RCIA team. It was also very near the shops, the post office, the library and numerous bus stops with buses heading in many different directions.

There were very many social events in the house and we joined in because we felt that if we were going to be there we had to be part of the Stannard Court community. We also had other contacts. Anne visited some of the more elderly and sick residents. A lovely lady who had had an implant to help her hearing, asked me to help her practise her hearing. We read some very good books together and finally became very good friends. Campion, who worked at Belmarsh Prison, continued her work. Anne went to the Jesuit Refugee Service and I continued my work of spiritual direction, some of my previous clients coming to Stannard Court and I also continued my visits to Wimbledon. Warm relationships were established, particularly at the social events we had. In that way I made a good friend and was introduced to the art club in the local Baptist church. So there were more contacts made. Each of us had a flat but we had frequent contacts and regularly prayed together and had a meal together. We had shopping expeditions together. When Anne sadly needed to move to Westgate, Sr. Anastasia moved into No. 69. Campion became very ill and was admitted to Lewisham hospital and then to Kings College for major surgery. She did not return to Stannard Court but went to Westgate where she died sadly just after a few months.

Then came the end. Anastasia and I were to move to Westgate. I was the last to move and a group of the residents arranged a lovely party for anyone in the house who cared to come. After that, one lady's cry was "No more sisters" and that suggests that the sisters had been valued and this experiment of a new foundation which had only lasted 8 years had had a good outcome."

Sister Damien O'Mahony

"I retired as a primary school Headteacher in summer 2003. During my sabbatical year I spent some time in Rome where I followed a course at Regina Mundi and did an intensive TEFL course which qualified me to teach English as a second language.

After some years as housekeeper in our Generalate in Rome and a spell in our convent in Ilford I joined the North-West Ursuline Cluster and moved to Wythenshawe. These years were interesting and rewarding. I became very involved in the Wythenshawe deanery. I was responsible for the children's liturgy in the parishes, prepared for Masses and baptisms in my parish and was available to support a variety of people. I felt very privileged to take communion to sick and lonely people. I was an active and supportive governor in a Primary and Secondary school. For many years I used my TEFL skills to support Ursuline Sisters from Poland and Croatia to improve their English.

For three years we ran Ursuline Links Day Camps for a week in the summer. Students from Ursuline schools in London spent a week in Wythenshawe helping to run the camps. They were a huge success and incredibly popular. Not only did the children enjoy the experiences of drama, music, flower arranging etc, and an exciting day's outing, the parents were full of praise. We had planned a Day Camp for 2020, but sadly the pandemic prevented it from going ahead.

I became unwell in 2014 so for a while my activities were curtailed. Now that Covid is mostly behind us I am able to be involved in the parish by doing the admin work for the gift aid scheme and I run the bi-monthly meetings of the SVP (I'm currently the President). I also support many people via phone calls."

We are proud of our tradition in education and pleased to find it continued in our schools today.
Influenced by the needs of our times our work is now more varied, as we seek to respond to the social, human and spiritual needs around us.

We are committed to working towards Peace, Justice, and Integrity of Creation.

Through Ursuline Links, our Youth Programme, we aim to deepen the prayer life of young people and offer them opportunities of service to the wider community.

We aim, with the help of those we meet, to make a difference and to make Christ's presence more known and felt.

"You have more need to serve others than to be served."
- St Angela Merici

Ursulines see ministry as a whole in which we are actively involved as a community, no matter how individual or specialised a sister's role. In the 51 years between 1962 and 2023 we have been 'shaken to our roots' as we faced many unexpected changes, challenges and demands. In this section as in PRAYER and COMMUNITY we see how different sisters have responded.

The past 50 years have seen much enriching educational change and development, which has been mirrored in our schools. In most cases these are now run under Diocesan management. In this part therefore, we look at Ministry under **Schools** and Widening Apostolate'.

Schools

Vatican II has already been described as a "Sea Change" As Sisters we were all familiar with every subtle nuance of each dotted plain chant note; "musical" sisters attended special courses in plain chant. Choir practices were weekly and every school girl had been drilled in at least Missa De Angelis for special feast day celebrations. Mass in English was greatly welcomed but suddenly we were faced with a musical desert. Several sisters accepted the challenge to turn their hand to "vernacular creativity" which saw us through much of this period but gradually this became a niche market. One certainly welcomed by Sr Margaret Lyth (John) who was responsible for liturgy at the Westgate Boarding School.

Development of Liturgy at Westgate School and Community

"When I went to Westgate in 1963 the liturgy was all in Latin, the hymn book was the Westminster Hymnal (I remember holidays spent patching them up to keep them in use) and the sisters said the Little Office of Our Lady in Latin.

Sister Margaret Lyth

With the Second Vatican Council came a loosening of liturgical reins and popular, easy-to- learn hymns were introduced. Gradually Catholic musicians, lay and clerical, began producing English versions of the Ordinary of the Mass and groups like the American St Louis Jesuits offered biblical texts to guitar music. Some of the pupils were skilled guitarists and singing at Sunday Mass grew in volume. Later, skilled piano pupils accompanied the singing on an electronic organ.

I got permission to use an English version of the O Salutaris and Tantum Ergo and later, with the help of Mrs Davies, the school's music teacher, well-known Anglican hymns from the Ancient and Modern Hymnal were introduced.

The Thomas More Pastoral Centre also began to create beautiful hymn melodies and words, and the reflective chants of Taize and Margaret Rizza also became part of our repertoire. Meanwhile, after 1972 the sisters began using the Divine Office Books in English and with the help of Mrs Davies we introduced simple psalm tones from the Anglican psalter. New hymn books were constantly being published and we took time to decide what we could afford to buy. Even today we still have some copies of the Westminster Hymnal which we use occasionally.

Vatican 2 and Religious Education

With Vatican 2 there was renewed energy in the catechetical field. Up to this point school religious education concentrated predominantly on Catholic beliefs, practice, ritual and conversions. Slowly our horizons widened as we began to look outwards. There were many young priests who captured Vatican II's enthusiasm, gave different style retreats, ran scripture courses and experimented with liturgies pared down to their fundamental core. As young nuns at that time we were very fortunate to have our House of Studies in London and several sisters in management who were open to this change.

This was reflected in schools with the introduction of new lively colourful RE Syllabuses particularly in primary schools and in the secondary schools by an O level/GCSE examination relevant to Catholic Schools and acceptable for university entry requirements. Catholic Social Teaching, hitherto locked up in the small print and encyclical language of Rerum Novarum and Quadragesima Anno, became a fresh reality. School retreats became less formal, and, in a variety of forms an annual opportunity for differing year groups.

Many convents and schools were involved in training catechists and providing them with a sound scriptural background. Wimbledon 6th formers continued teaching catechetics at the South Wimbledon parish for many years. Provision was also strong at Forest Gate as this was an area in which the Windrush Generation settled and the Catholic population increased significantly. There was therefore a shortage of Catholic School places. Forest Gate set up a Saturday School for catechism, staffed by nuns and Catholic Laity. It ran until well into the Eighties. Religious Education is a legal right in English schools and sisters were invited to run classes for the Catholics in four Local Secondary State schools, a practice that continued until the re-organisation to Comprehensive Education in 1972.

Schools Ministry

Sister Mary Murphy

Sister Mary was very happy as an English teacher. She had wide experience throughout the province and was popular with her pupils. Rula Lenska met her as an English teacher at Westgate and she invited her as a guest, when appearing on the Eamon Andrews "This is your life!".
Mary had spells of teaching at Westgate, Wimbledon and Forest Gate. She was one of the first to join St Bede's Catholic High school at

Chester, when the Ursuline Convent there gradually closed. She then became Head of Westgate Boarding School where she remained until her retirement in 1995.

BERNIE O'GRADY, her deputy has this to say of her headship years.
"Sr Mary Murphy - a name that is synonymous with the Ursuline Convent School for Girls Westgate. I first met this lovely lady in June 1985, when I attended an interview for the post of Geography teacher. I was immediately struck by her warm welcome, her enthusiasm and her kindness. If I had to choose one word to sum up Sr Mary, it would be 'kind'. Sr Mary took a full and genuine interest in everyone in her care at the school, whether they were students or employees. She had wonderful rapport with parents and the school was always a welcoming place. She took particular interest in students on assisted places and always ensured that they were able to fully participate in everything the school had to offer. Sr Mary gave staff great freedom to explore teaching beyond the classroom and she was a great supporter of field trips and arts events.

Teddy

She believed in developing grounded, well-rounded young women of the future and that success in life was not measured by academic excellence alone, but also by the joy of music or drama, skills on the games fields or in debates and above all in service to others. She also had a wonderful way of bringing her staff together and we have so many memories of happy social events such as American Suppers and end of term celebrations.

The boarders held Sr Mary in very high regard - she was the boss but her office door was always open and they knew they could turn to her when times were difficult. She had good humour and a great presence - she added gravitas to any occasion.

On a personal level, I will always be grateful to Sr Mary for her kindness to me and my family and I know that many past members of staff would say the same thing. She was always supportive and interested - she helped me find accommodation when I first arrived, shared my joy when I got married and when my children were born but she was also there to listen and help when times were difficult, times of loss and illness. We, as her staff loved her and appreciated her kindness and it was always a joy to meet her in more recent times and to reminisce on happy times and past pupils, staff and friends at the Ursuline Convent School."

Mary and Westgate were one. She spent most of her retirement there, much of it, as Sister in charge of our Nursing Home in Lourdes. As well as the Sisters, Teddy the cat, became a day boarder being driven back to his home each evening chauffeured by Sr. Mary!

Sister Mary Charles Conway was born in Scotland in April 1927, she was the youngest of four girls in a close-knit, loving family. She attended the Mercy convent from the age of 5 to 17, which was briefly interrupted, when the school where her father taught was evacuated and the rest of the family joined him.

When she completed her schooling, she went to Teacher Training in Glasgow and studied Maths, her favourite subject! After training, she taught for 5 years in Glasgow and then entered the Ursulines at Westgate. A surprising choice, but she felt that to join the Mercy Sisters and remain in Glasgow would be too confining and she had an aunt who was an Ursuline Sister.

She settled quickly and her great gift of service, which became a hallmark, was soon evident. Her first post was at Ilford Preparatory School, but as a highly gifted Maths teacher with a good singing voice, she found herself on the Ursuline circuit. She served in Ilford, Westgate, Greenwich, Lourdes, Wimbledon and Forest Gate. She was a teacher, Prioress, bursar, as well as a carer for the frail and sick sisters at Greenwich. The uprooting and resettling she experienced must have been a challenge. Mary Charles found religious life fulfilling and enriching. She loved teaching Maths and was highly successful in it. She didn't seek out mathematical stars, but became excellent at reducing complex issues to ordinary language. And there are countless struggling students, who can still look up at the ceiling and configure Pythagoras as she taught them.

"I remember the first time I met Sister Mary Charles was when we had a look at the school after being given a place there. She said "I am Sister Mary Charles, I am your form tutor, maths teacher, RE teacher and I love maths". My reply was "I am Denise Pittman and I hate maths." She said "we will get on great and I will make sure you love maths". With her help, I tried my best! She had a great sense of humour, was very strict and very fair."

Mary Charles joined the Forest Gate community in 1998. By that time she was retired. She became an expert in DIY when the community turned some spare rooms into teacher flats. She also shared in many new Justice and Peace ventures and took part in the 'Edinburgh drop the debt' and the London 'No to the Iraq War' marches. She was also very much part of the Ursuline Olympic involvement.

Throughout her life she remained firmly Scottish, a Glaswegian, a Celtic supporter and a member of St Aloysius Parish, which like her Scottish accent, always remained alive for her. She will always be remembered for the positive and kind contribution she made to the communities and schools where she served.

"I have lots of fond memories of her with her maths groups. There are so many children who benefited from her patience."

Sr. Mary Charles died on 7th March 2022.

Sister Beatrice Garnett

"I was fortunate to return from tertianship at a time when St Ursula's School Greenwich which was then the Inner London Education Authority. It was "getting its act together" as a girls' comprehensive with a wide catchment. This embraced the generously resourced extensive London Docklands Development Area, new developments for the Millennium, Docklands Light Railway and the ambition to put in place the foundations for future technology that would enable the area to challenge the traditional prestige of the City of London in international finance.

In St Ursula's there was a Geography teaching vacancy coming and I was in the right place at the right time: a space in a comprehensive staffroom of strong ability, loyalty and a cooperative spirit. We knew how lucky we were to be there.

It is difficult and interesting to look back on all the local controversies where, as geographers, we had a contribution to offer. The area included the largest acreage of docks, now obsolete, surrounded by dereliction of bombed warehouse sites, polluted land and questions as to how development should take place. And younger people, my pupils, were listened to as we were able to take part in meetings and even televised discussions on planning, the environment, flood prevention, the future O2. All this amidst the historical riches and background of the Tudor palace and Henry VIII: without forgetting that out of our windows we could see the site of the world Zero Longitude overlooking the Thames, a major highway of times past.

For teaching Geography, Inner London had useful, and free offers, including centres where staff could train for mountain leadership so that we could then take groups. I can remember having reached the summit of Snowdon with a group of London A level students when the clouds cleared and the view was beyond even my wildest hopes. All the long way down a student stuck beside me, repeating every other moment "Isn't it beautiful, Sister?"

So, I look back on my years teaching in comprehensive schools; we had some outstanding staff, great companions and a lot to learn. What more can be said, except a profound "Thank you" for the gifts of God and Ursuline vocation."

Sister Alice Montgomery - Ursuline College Westgate

"In September 1995, the Ursuline Convent School in Westgate, accepted nearly 200 boys from the recently closed St Augustine's School in Westgate. Hence the Ursuline School became co-educational and was from then on known as the Ursuline College. It was a courageous move by the Ursulines, but made sense as the small private boarding and day school had experienced a drop in numbers.

The school had to be rapidly adapted to be ready to take on the additional male students including additional mobile classrooms, changing rooms and toilets. For the first year, the classes from Year 7 to 11 were taught in single sex groupings. Later that changed as the College adapted itself. In order to facilitate the additional need for boarding places, a small hotel on the seafront called Edgewater, was purchased. This was just a ten-minute walk from the school.

However, it was clear to the management of the school that there needed to be a more realistic approach to the future. At this time, the government of the day was accepting private schools to apply to become state funded if they were able to demonstrate that they were of a high enough standard. As a Catholic school, this meant also being accepted by the diocese to be publicly funded.

It was agreed by the governing body that the then headteacher, Sr Alice Montgomery and the Provincial as the legal representative, Sr. Frances Oakley, would approach the Archbishop of Southwark, to ask permission to become a diocesan school. After some debate this was agreed.

In addition to this, the school had to apply to the government to become a voluntary aided school. An inspection was held to make sure the school was of the right standard. This was successful. In September 1998, the Ursuline College became a Catholic, co-educational, comprehensive and voluntary aided school for students aged 11 to 18 under the Diocese of Southwark. It was no longer a private school.

After another two years, the boarding part of the school had to be closed as this could not receive government funding.

In September 1998, the school had approximately 450 students. From then on it began to grow rapidly and permission was received to build an additional teaching block called St. Ursula's. This three-floor building housed general teaching rooms in addition to a Science floor and a dedicated technology area. It was opened by Archbishop Michael Bowen on 16th February 2001.

The College eventually became a Sports Specialist College and a large sports hall called St. Joseph's, was opened by Bishop John Hine on 6th July, 2007.

The school presently has over 970 students coming from all over Thanet and beyond.

A central part of the site has always been the Chapel which has provided the opportunity for over 200 students at a time to experience liturgy and year group assemblies. It has rightly been considered a great asset in a Catholic school.

One of the enduring features of the location of the Ursuline College, has been it close proximity to the sea enjoyed by staff, students and Ursuline Sisters. Its simple and unspoilt charm continues to this day."

Widening Apostolate

Some of our new ventures were undertaken by retired sisters who made career changes. As pensions became available at about 60 many sisters felt they still had abundant energy and became involved in a variety of new ventures involved in parishes, justice and peace and local issues. Below you can read about some of these activities

Sister Veronica Gissing

"I first came across AIDS when I was doing my spiritual direction course. I had someone who was desperately upset that her brother was dying of AIDS. She didn't really know what it was and neither did I. He was in the United States and she couldn't let the rest of the family know. I realised then, that this was something awful. A few months later I was in San Francisco, the Castle area and it was a huge problem. When I went a year later, I was at Mass and the priest said "Now let's pray for the next group of people who are going to die this week". That's

how it was, all the young in the Castle area dying of AIDS. Whilst there, I met an Ursuline Sister who was in charge of the AIDS response in one of the New York hospitals and when I came home I thought that I must do something but didn't know where to start in England.

I phoned someone who put me in touch with an Anglican Franciscan who was in charge. So, I went to see him, a lovely man. He said he had become involved following a trip to the States where he met a wonderful sister who ran a centre for AIDS sufferers very early on, and it was one of our Ursuline Sisters. Our stories had crossed paths. An Ursuline had helped him and now he was going to help me.

AIDS in London was divided between the East and West. The West End had all the facilities, they were well educated, had money and the East was poor. Many of the people I met in the East came from difficult upbringings and I got the sense that they had never known love and now they were outcasts in the area. We had a place which we called Route 15- it was on the route 15 bus which many had to take to get up to the London hospitals. It was useful and no one in the local area knew what it was- so it was safe.

At the centre there was a quiet room with a peaceful waterfall. The group met, talked and had a Tuesday night supper with yards and yards of jam roly poly and custard. They loved it!

Mostly we had young people but also a few wonderful middle-aged people who of course, died quite quickly. We had many funerals, lots of different types of funerals. There was a lovely Catholic priest who was chaplain at The London Hospital who was very involved with the AIDS response, something that surprised many. He had a terrific sense of humour and a great Oxford accent which stood out in the chaotic East End! He saw many of them off. Always on December 1st, a day to remember those affected by AIDS, we would hold a deeply spiritual remembrance service, with prayers and candles to remember those we had lost.

We saw life and met lots of different people. Michael, whom I liked, was out of the Air Force but was very naughty. He didn't do anything I asked him to do. He would hang around on a Tuesday night and not help. One day I was with him alone for a while and he said "I spent my money on a Bible this week, it's quite good in parts" I asked him what part he was reading. He said "I couldn't start at the beginning and go through it like that but some parts are very good". He was often buried in the corner reading his Bible. Gradually he got to know the priest who was Chaplain at the hospital and at one Easter Vigil when he was very ill, he was received into the church. When I visited him in Guys Hospital he told me that he had been given six weeks to live. I asked him how he felt about it and he replied "If what you and I think is true and what we believe, then I want to get there". And he did."

Sister Vianney Connolly

What led me to give 25 years as a volunteer for CAFOD? I think initially it was a question of justice. I realised through my education at St Angela's that there was a third world and a first world as they were called and the third world had a rough time. It was illustrated for me at a dinner where there were 10 people in a circle where someone was handing out plates of food. Two plates were divided by eight people and the other two people got eight plates. And they said this is the situation in our world at the moment; 20% of the world's population are consuming 80% of the world's resources and 80% of the world's population have access to 20%. I thought that this shouldn't continue and knew that CAFOD were engaged in trying to make the world a fairer place- this excited me!

When I was asked by the parish priest in North Wales to take over their CAFOD group that was dying out, I gladly took it on and when I was asked, having come out of school, to share with another Order the setting up of a CAFOD resource centre for the diocese of Wrexham. I was happy to get going. CAFOD for me, described by Cardinal Hume as 'a conspiracy of love' was just the kind of organisation I wanted to be part of. It brought a lot of friendship, it brought a lot of struggle but I loved its littleness- its little beginnings. The four women meeting in their kitchen and throwing out a challenge to every catholic family in England and Wales. They responded to an appeal that came from, across the other side of the world. They cared that the only Mother and Baby Home on the island of Dominica, in the Caribbean, should not close for lack of funds. They challenged every family to go without a main meal or eat something less expensive on the first Friday of Lent and give the money they saved to CAFOD. They were hoping to raise £500 but raised £5000. That was the little beginning and CAFOD itself, when it was established in London, began in a basement in SOHO with volunteers.

I loved CAFOD's spirit. It was a question of partnerships- you were giving and receiving and you received far more than you gave. It was like reaching across the world to grasp another's hand. There was never any sign of patronising, this was equality- giving and receiving and listening to what a community needed in order to improve life. I did not work on my own of course, I worked with so many different people. Lovely friendships developed over the years and not just amongst Catholics. When CAFOD moved into campaigning for justice, they were guided by 'Populorum Progressio', the encyclical of Pope Paul VI, that said we owed it to God to develop the whole of ourselves and this meant all peoples, not just privileged individuals. Once CAFOD established its emergency response department it began to work with other NGOs (Non Government Organisations) to form the Disasters

Emergency Committee (DEC) so that there was a sharing of skills and what was needed.

So, when I look back it was a conspiracy of love and it was the work of the Holy Spirit. It turned me inside out without me realising, I was looking outwards, sideways and upwards in prayer. It was all very good for the heart and I think I was so enriched through our campaigning in London, Birmingham, Scotland and Europe. I am extremely grateful."

Sister Antonia Ashpole

"People ask me why I joined the Ursulines as I never wanted to teach. I tell them you have to ask God that! It was the Ursulines I was called to and where I always felt at home. But teaching is what they did, so I taught for two years and was thoroughly miserable. I ended up as a lab technician in the local Catholic school for nine years but was always given the sick or elderly nuns to look after and if they died I hadn't a clue what to do.

Three of my sisters were nurses by this stage, so I thought maybe I should ask to do nursing – that is always useful in a community. Things had changed a lot for us and I was given permission to do nurse training. At the end of the three years my six weeks on the maternity ward had touched my soul and I asked if I could train to be a midwife. This was also agreed to, so 18 months later I was a midwife. It was the

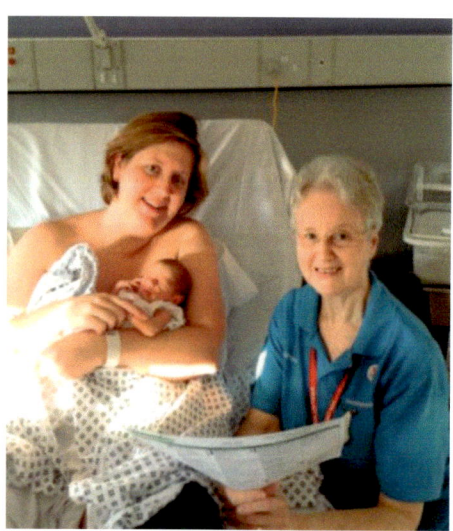

best thing I ever did, but it also carried a lot of responsibility. I worked for 4 years on the wards but then asked to go into the community. As a community midwife you do EVERYTHING – antenatal clinics, deliveries and postnatal care and there is much more continuity of patients. It was a wonderful job and my favourite experience was looking after a new mum postnatally. Then, when she got pregnant again I looked after her all the way through the pregnancy, delivered her and visited postnatally. Later I had a student and the mum got pregnant again and I supervised my student all the way through this lady's care and the delivery.

Of course there are always sad events when looking after pregnant women.

Because I lived and worked in an area with a large Asian community, my 'mums' were mostly Asian. It was a great privilege to enter their homes and care for the mum and baby and to meet the rest of the family. Sometimes an older child would ask me to take the baby back to the hospital!

After I retired I worked voluntarily on the postnatal ward at a local hospital and also had a Mums and Babies group in the convent.

I never had a connection with St Angela through 'Education' but I know that through my service as a midwife she would have been very proud of me."

Sister Gwyn Richards

"In the early seventies, the Hierarchy asked leaders of Religious Congregations to release sisters to work full time setting up diocesan services for deaf people. I was asked, and although it was not easy at first, this really was a major step forward in my religious life, trying to bring the Good News to people, many of whom had little knowledge of Jesus Christ.

I had a year's training and then in 1978 began the pioneering work in Brentwood Diocese for nearly twenty years. I was employed and supported by the diocese and also by our network of workers through the national Catholic Deaf Association. I soon found out that profoundly deaf people felt not only left out from the life of the church but also from society in general, so it was challenging to set up appropriate services. The Ursuline Community, kindly gave the ground floor of a house in Ilford so St Angela's Centre for Deaf People was established. I organised church services in sign language and tried to get deaf people involved in their local parishes, which was very difficult. I got grants for a few deaf people to be trained as sign language tutors at Durham University. I trained catechists to teach children their faith and support the parents and some of these have remained friends for many years. I also campaigned nationally for local authorities to put on sign language classes and to get interpreters trained for work in courts and some hospital consultations as a start and then in society generally.

Fr Gerald Gostling was inspired to train and although he was a busy parish priest we worked together. He signed Masses and I gradually trained a deaf choir. Deaf people signing while the hearing ones sang. Together we took children on catechetical residential holiday camps with at least one teacher of the deaf and accompanied deaf adults to Lourdes. An especially memorable occasion was when I joined the Brentwood Catholic Youth Service on their pilgrimage to Lourdes by coach, taking a few deaf teenagers at a time, serving the sick. A young girl in a wheelchair remarked about a deaf helper "He's never heard a word his mother has said!" and the young helper responded saying he was lucky because he could walk and run. It was a very good experience for both the hearing and the deaf youth.

Lunch clubs for deaf people flourished, and we had a similar lunch club for hard of hearing people, as well as a lip-reading class for them. Day camps were enabled by the Ilford Ursuline School providing their playground and dining hall. We worked with people of all cultures and faiths for the social activities. All this was only achieved through the hard work of many workers and volunteers, some of whom were experts at getting funding from various sources, notably BBC Children in Need. It was a most enjoyable life and I learnt a lot from the experience."

Sister Anastasia Nolan

"I always like to boast about having been in prison for 20 years! I was part of the chaplaincy team at Styal women's prison near Wythenshawe, Cheshire. I would go to the prison Monday, Wednesday, Friday and Saturday to speak to the women about their faith and run groups in the chapel. The prison had women of many different faiths- Catholic, Anglican, Muslim, Sikhs etc. It didn't matter to me what faith they were, I would always ask them about it. When I speak of my time working at the prison, I cannot stop talking about the care and structure the women had. It didn't matter where the women came from, what religion they were, they were all cared for and their religion honoured. There were no cells, there were houses with about 15 women in each house. They had their own rooms apart from on rare occasions when two women had to share. There was a centre for the sick and a mother and baby unit.

The women had to be up in the morning, strip their beds, have breakfast and go to work. Everyone had to work. They grew all their own vegetables and there was a place to grow flowers. The people who worked there were wonderful. There was an art teacher, gardeners who showed them how to plant etc, a needlework room where they would make curtains and a laundry. Whatever they were good at, they were encouraged to do it. Some women arrived at the prison pregnant. They would go to Wythenshawe hospital to have their babies and then they were nursed back at the prison.

We had a beautiful chapel and each religion would be given a day to use it. When the women came up to the chapel, we would have scripture readings, the rosary and on a Friday, a play and pray for the mothers and babies. There was more play than prayer but I didn't mind! Mass was celebrated on a Saturday morning. I never felt threatened by the women. Of course, there were disagreements among them but I would go along and say "Oh girls what's this disturbance about? You are keeping me away from my prayers!" It woud always ok if you kept it light-hearted with them.

A funny story was when I was getting on the bus going into Manchester and I heard someone shout "Sr Anastasia! We were in prison together!" and all the heads on the bus turned to look at me and people were moving their bags and shuffling away from me.

I look back at those years fondly. It was a wonderful time for me, I loved it. "

Sister Catherine Kelly

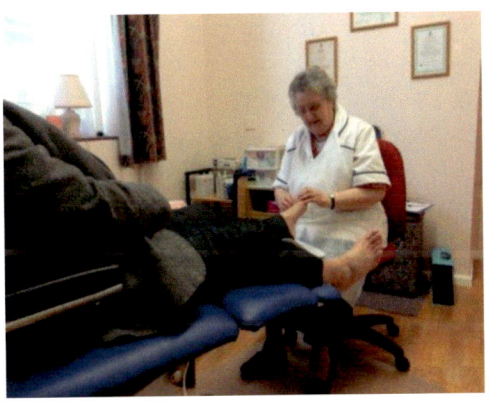

"What on earth does one do when retiring after 41 years of teaching? This was my dilemma. I knew that I would have to do something that would keep me active, there was no way I could vegetate! After much prayer and deliberation, I felt that Foot Care was a possible opening, knowing the relief it would bring people. I investigated various possibilities and felt that full Chiropody training was too much at my age as that included surgery. I discovered that there was a course for Foot Health Professionals, which involved basic foot health care i.e. cutting nails, removing corns etc. The course was online! You might ask how that was possible? All the medical study was done 'online' with an examination at the end of each section. Then, when the college was satisfied that you had reached the required standard, they would call you for a two- week residential, practical course where you learnt how to use the various instruments and meet all the various foot problems one is likely to encounter. For me this has been a wonderful journey.

Most of my patients are elderly and to see the relief when they have completed a visit is such a joy. Some have cried when they have found that they can walk without pain. Some of my patients come to the clinic in the convent, others I visit in their homes.

Once a month I visit two Homeless Care Centres and this is my favourite encounter as the men and women I help are always so grateful and greet me like a friend. You can imagine the state of their feet!

I thank the Lord that He showed me this opening."

Sister Elizabeth Campbell and Sister Una McCreesh

"When Sister Elizabeth and I retired we were aware of the great need for English in the Ursuline Order. Sisters came from many provinces to all our convents at differing times in the summer to learn English; we decided to rationalise this and run an annual summer school at Westgate. The first of these was in 1995. It was generally only possible to send one or two sisters per province, but the need was great and we soon found ourselves invited to individual provinces to run courses there, especially for younger nuns. As a result, we became world travellers, visiting many countries in Europe and many further afield, including Thailand, Indonesia, Brazil and China and finally Ethiopia.

Ethiopia was in fact something of a surprise as it was not part of the Roman Union. Sister Askalamariam came to England to follow a Fashion and Design Course, which happened to be at Greenwich. She stayed in our convent and she invited us to go and teach their younger sisters. There are many Ethiopian languages and English was rapidly becoming the medium of secondary education.

Ethiopia proved an experience like no other. Our first visit was in 2005 and our swan song in 2018. We arrived at Addis Ababa "state of the art" airport. where we were met by the sisters and driven on the six-lane highway. After about a mile it became a track and about an hour later we reached Shola where the postulants and novices at that time lived. The next morning, we went to an early Mass at the local Benedictine monastery nearby. My first memories are of a rough track, lots of people, several sheep, goats, heavily laden donkeys, sunshine and vitality! Each morning we taught all the postulants, and sisters who had come specially for the course, and the kindergarten teachers after school, and that became our constant pattern for several years.

We also got to know the sisters well and a great rapport grew up between us which is still alive today. The sisters were founded from Gandino in Italy, 75 years earlier.

Ethiopia is a predominantly religious country with Catholics, Orthodox and Muslims. From the outset, the sisters did not aim at conversion but at the betterment of people, especially women. Their first venture was to found a needlework school for women. This, like their orphanages and clinics, was open to all faiths. By 2000, the Italian sisters had returned to Italy leaving behind 48 indigenous sisters and 20 plus in training who had clearly caught the spirit of their founders and totally lived among their people. This impressed us greatly and we felt drawn to help in whatever ways we could.

Ways came much more quickly than we expected. The Novice Mistress asked us to help complete an application to Hilton Hotels to fund training. When we read the small print, it was clear that training was not on offer but they could fund women's projects and orphanages. Nothing daunted us, we found ourselves flying north to Wukro in Tigray - where the sisters had both a women's group and an orphanage.

The poverty was great. So was the heat! The glass in the curtainless windows was painted and like everyone else we had half a bucket of water per day for our personal needs! But there was no doubt at all what a difference these sisters were making and how well they knew and respected their people. We sent off a successful application form to the Hilton and got a grant for several years for both the women and orphans.

We came home wiser and enriched by our experience. We clearly had to do what we could and so ade appeals to our schools, parishes, and charities and had the joys of seeing Ethiopia grow and transform beyond recognition in 13 years. We are grateful to many who listened and contributed to our appeals. Above all we are grateful for the friendship and understanding that has grown between our two countries. Saddened as we all are by the current state of war, we continue to keep close contact, to pray and give what support we can."

Sister Emmanuel Bali

Very many years ago in the House of Studies it was the eve of Emmanuel's Craft exhibition for her final Teacher's exam and the provincial happened to be visiting. She came to recreation where everyone seemed to be diligently occupied and decided to ask what each one was doing; the first sister said she was doing something for sister Emmanuel, the second one said the same, the third said the same and so on around the circle. There was one abstainer, Sister Audrey who happened to be putting finishing touches to an item for her own final presentation!

The persuasive manner, generally accompanied by an air of secrecy, and her ability for eleventh hour rescues remained hallmarks throughout Emmanuel's life. She liked variety and change and slipped seamlessly from career to career, generally preferring to engage with those on the margins.

Emmanuel often worked in teams. She had some stints in school but Heads generally like timetables and predictability, so this did not remain her principal field! She worked with Westgate boarders at weekends, running popular Duke of Edinburgh Award Courses. She spent some years working with The Fountain Trust distributing religious tapes when that became a popular medium. She was also sometime a welfare leader at the Ursuline Wimbledon and was noted for her kindness.

She worked for several years with another Sister at St Patrick's Soho where they had a project offering support to Au Pairs, who often found themselves lonely or in placement difficulties. Emmanuel always worked hard and enjoyed what she did. It was our intention to interview her about this ground-breaking work but unfortunately, she became ill before we could do so.

However one sister has sent this memory and it seems an appropriate end point as Emmanuel worked with Bob Faricy frequently. "Three of us Ursulines went to a retreat, I think in Leeds, run by a team. Sr Emmanuel's part was to run the shop of books and CDs. Being Emmanuel, she was often engaged with people, praying or listening to their stories. After a day, Fr Bob announced that the team would take it in turns to run the bookshop and leave Sr Emmanuel to do the things she did best. Their acceptance of Emmanuel's giftedness and their love and support of her as she is, was the biggest lesson I took away from that retreat."

Sr Emmanuel died on 7th March 2023 at Chestnut Manor care home.

Sister Anne-Marie Gardiner - Service in Rome

I was born and brought up in Scotland and had never met any Ursulines. After I finished my studies I joined the civil service and worked with what was then the Ministry of Agriculture, working mainly in the North of England and latterly in the South. I enjoyed my work enormously and advanced through the usual promotions but felt at the same time that God was calling me to a different kind of service though I wasn't sure what.

In 1987 on the weekend of the 'hurricane' in the South East of England, I went to a 'Choice Weekend', a residential course for young people making choices in their lives and there I met my first Ursuline by chance in the book shop. She would send me leaflets about other weekends but I was never able to go. Eventually though, I asked to speak with her and became interested in joining the Ursulines as a way of deeper service.

After my novitiate and further studies, I began to teach, finding myself increasingly interested in those who had behavioural difficulties. I began training in counselling and psychotherapy with the intention to serve in school settings. This I did, mainly in Ursuline secondary schools, some primary schools and also in a primary school as part of the "Place to Be" initiative. I also built up a private practice.

I was happy doing this very necessary service and getting to know pupils at a deeper level. However, I was called to a very different kind of service after a few years. I was asked to be Provincial in England and then after only a year or so, I was elected to the General Council in Rome by our General Chapter. This required me to

In this role I have learnt much about the service given by the Ursuline sisters throughout the world. Some are deeply involved in the education system in their countries, others in pastoral, social and outreach work. Our sisters do great work serving those in need. The older sisters have a lively interest in and pray for the needs of those working in a more hands-on way. However, what is common to all the work being done, is the deep willingness to serve people and to meet the needs presented. Sisters see their availability to local communities as a way of following the gospel and the teaching of St Angela.

What has been a joy is that, wherever I go in the world, I have been welcomed and felt at home in each community, feeling a strong sense of the spirit of St Angela. Even when we come from different cultures and don't share a common spoken language our common life of prayer and service unites us.

"Have engraved on your mind and heart all your dear daughters"
-St Angela Merici

Money Matters

Sister Maureen Moloney, Provincial Treasurer

Looking back over the past 100 years we cannot but be made aware of the tremendous help successive British governments have given to the Church, and hence to us as Ursulines, most especially for education. We have also benefited greatly since 1948 from free healthcare and over the years the pension schemes.

As we continue to look back we have other people and organisations to thank for their sound advice, support or financial aid. As Ursulines we too have been proactive in our decisions and responsibilities regarding the use of our finances. It is impossible to record all the many rich ways/decisions we have taken on our journey for our finances and for our resources but a few notable ones are mentioned here.

Professional advice

Our accountant of many decades ago, Mr Godfrey of Godfrey, Lord and Co. (father of Sr Anne Godfrey) strongly advised us to make sure that all our Sisters paid into the National Insurance Scheme for state pensions in later life, as well as paying into Occupational Pensions. Early on this meant a great sacrifice for the province as many communities had large debts to the banks in those early days as a result of all the school buildings post the 1944 Education Act.

Bequests and Legacies

In recording various aspects of our financial status and accountability it would be very important for us as Ursulines of the English Province to express our heartfelt thanks for those who, over the years, have remembered us in their wills by leaving us a **bequest.** In recent years these bequests have helped us implement some of our plans for our "downsizing" as we move into our next phase of Ursuline life in England. We have also been able to be more generous in our support of Ursuline Links, needy Ursuline provinces, CAFOD and Justice and Peace issues.

Ursuline Common Trust & Sharing Fund (CTSF)

This fund was set up as a legal entity by the Roman Union Ursulines and signed into life on 15th September 2010. It has as its main objects: To produce a large, varied, international portfolio, which should give good returns to the provinces and communities of Ursulines around the world who invest some of their finances.

To gift 20% of the profits each year to the Generalate INSIEME fund, for Ursulines in need, be it for formation, education, health needs, structural works, or for major catastrophes etc. Each Province can bid for financial help for special needs we might have. We have benefitted from it for some Ursuline Links projects.

I was on the Commission, working in Rome for the setting up of the CTSF, from 2007 to 2010, remaining a member of the commission and a Trustee of the fund until 2019. I remember vividly that I was due to meet Pope Benedict in England on 15th September 2010 but was summoned to Rome just a few days before this in order to sign the Ursuline CTSF into being on the very day Pope Benedict was meeting representatives of religious at St Mary's University Strawberry Hill!

Ethical Investments

As a Province we have always been aware of our responsibility to invest ethically. Our investments are necessarily handled by professional firms, but guided by the Ursuline Trustees' investment policy which we present to them for implementation. The policy is regularly updated in order to "capture" the new ways exploitation comes into our lives and the planet we inhabit.

We hold a small sum of money in the TRIODOS BANK. This is an ethical bank in its own right and it uses the capital to finance micro-projects, mainly in developing countries. Our own Justice and Peace and Integrity of Creation (JPIC) group over the years has been the main conscience of the province and we are all helped by the many International, National and Church groups focusing on the educational aspects of JPIC and this supports the Trustees' knowledge when upgrading our financial investment policy.

The present Pope, Francis, has led the way for the whole Church, if not the whole world, to be more aware of our need to care for the planet earth. The most recent international meeting of Ursulines has been focused on a study of our ongoing responsibility as an Order to integrate our learning with action. Much study of the topics was done in our communities prior to that gathering albeit often on Zoom due to Covid still being active around the world!

The CTSF ASSET MANAGERS are a flagship example in the research they do to make sure the investments mirror the ethical stance the Ursulines require …we are particularly grateful for the research the Netherlands Investment Managers do on our behalf, and that in turn educates us along the way.

Charity Status

The Charity of the Roman Union of the Order of St Ursula came into being on 15th September 1965. This meant that each sister signed a covenant that henceforth all their income would be paid directly to the Trust and as a result we would be exempt from tax. This tax rebate was given on the understanding that we would care for our sisters in their old age and to support our apostolic works. In recent years there has been an opportunity for Charities to move to a new type of Charity called a Charitable Incorporated Organisation (CIO). As the province moves into the later stages of completion there are added advantages for us to be a CIO. So, with the invaluable help of our professional collaborators, the Charity of the Roman Union of the Order of St Ursula changed its legal status into a CIO at 23.59 p.m. on 30th September 2020.

In setting up this new Charity we took the opportunity to appoint some "lay" Trustees, since, until then, all Trustees had been Ursulines of the English Province. The word "lay" is used in this instance for anyone not an Ursuline of the English Province. This is an example of how we have been working towards greater delegation.

Other collaborators over many, many years have worked together with the Ursulines of this Province: our Accountants, Bank Managers, Chartered Surveyors, Insurance Brokers, and Solicitors. These professional groups have worked hard on behalf of Religious in general, often putting on seminars or presentations to support our own ongoing formation. The Provincial Bursars' Association annual meeting (under the aegis of the Conference of Religious) adds to the rich diversity of support we have had over the years.

The Roman Union and Us

We are pleased that one hundred years ago our sisters chose, no doubt with a wing and a prayer, to join the Roman Union. This meant we could benefit from life in different communities and schools, get to know other sisters in our province and, as an international order in other parts of the world. As with any organisation, there are rules and regulations that chafe and the inevitable grumbles, that nobody understands our particular situation. But, there are two aspects that outweigh all our gripes! Our year of International Tertianship, and our direct experience of life in other parts of the world.

Tertianship

This is a sabbatical year of renewal, roughly ten years after our final profession. We spend time at the Generalate in Rome, sharing our religious life with sisters from other provinces and with no specific apostolic commitment. Tertianships were run in French and English and often with a third group from a minority language. For the second 6 months, it has increasingly become customary to use this time for service in another province. Sisters greatly value this period of renewal and remember it for life, and the lasting friends they made during it.

International Experience

We appreciate our ability to welcome sisters from other provinces to spend varying lengths of time living with us and vice versa. Present day life makes all of us aware of our global interconnectedness and our need to appreciate and understand each other. There are Roman Union convents in thirty four countries and the red dots on the maps below show the "Ursuline Homes" abroad, that our current English Province sisters have visited. Unfortunately, we don't have a comparable map to hand to show where the many sisters who have visited us came from, but we have been very enriched by them.

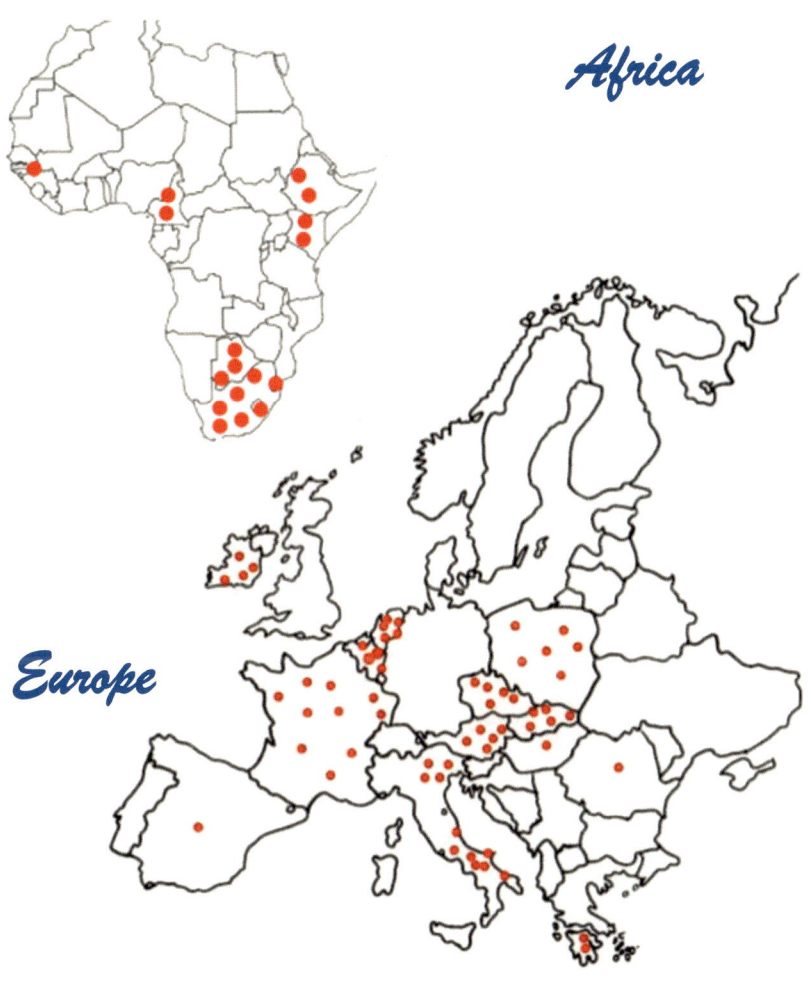

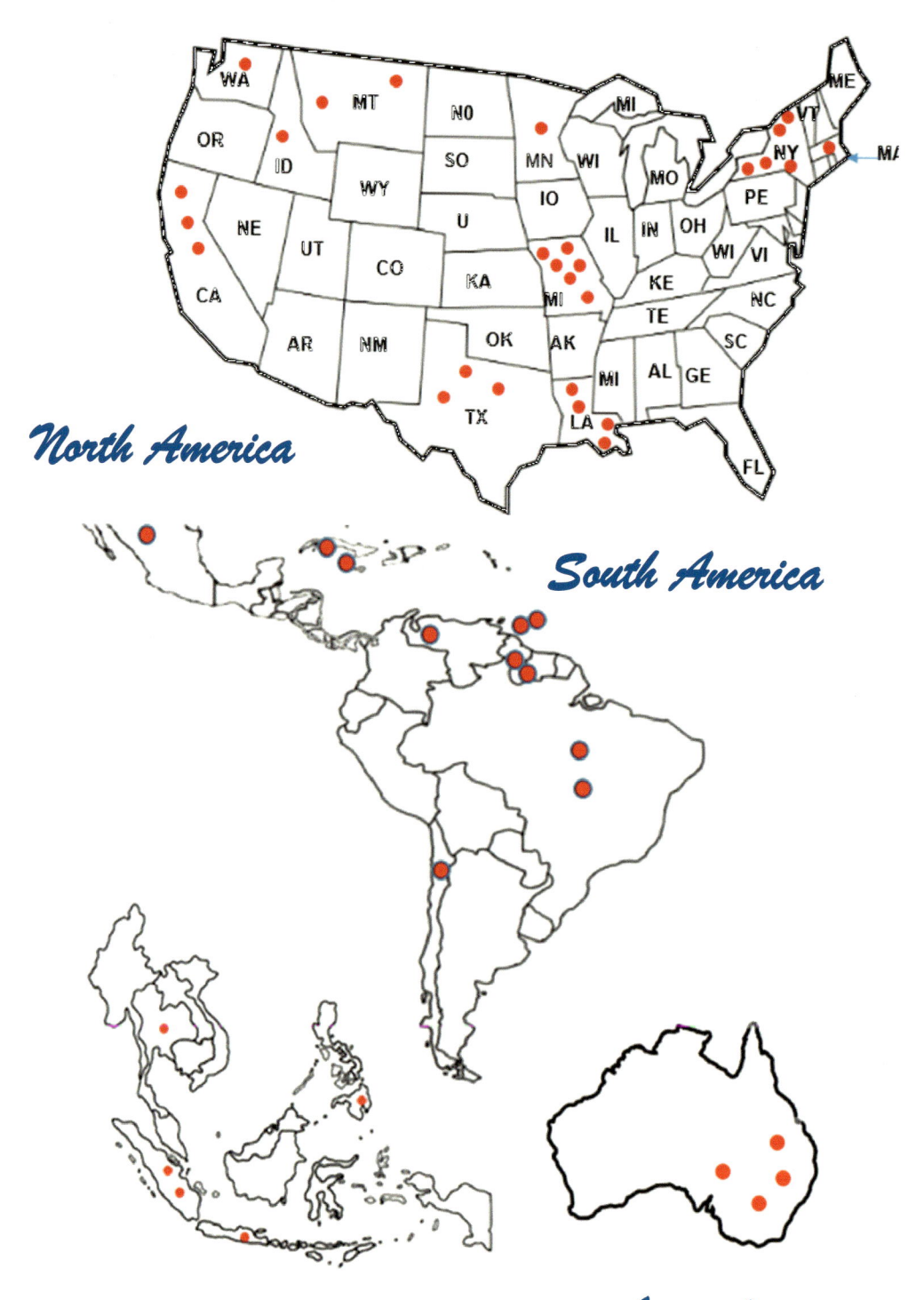

People Places Events

Movers and Shakers

Throughout our 100 years in the Roman Union, the English Province has a rich history to celebrate and be proud of. This chapter is dedicated to a selection of remarkable stories of our sisters.

Mother Angela Boord

As you will see from our introduction we have confined personal contributions to those sisters alive in 2022, when we began to shape this book. Every Sister by her daily life and personal commitment has contributed to our 100 years story, but, as in any organisation there are leaders, movers and shakers, who through personal talent and the circumstances of history are especially significant. There are several we could include here, but we have chosen **Sister Angela Boord** in particular; she lived to be 97 and achieved many amazing things, but above all she is known personally to all of the sisters alive today, as she was the elder 'stateswoman' at the House of Studies at Parkside 1956- 1970.

Sister Mary Angela, Evelyn Mary Maud, was born in 1887. Aged 10 she and her sister went to a convent boarding school on the outskirts of Paris. It was her first encounter with Catholicity and she was impressed. Ever a fast mover, by November the following year she had become a Catholic and 21st November, the feast of our Lady's Presentation, remained a 'Red Letter Day' for the rest of her life.

At age 14 she returned to England and became the first boarder at Wimbledon Ursuline School, which was just beginning. Two pupils, Monica and Ellie Hare were sent from Forest Gate to join her. Mother Angela and Ellie became lifelong friends, visiting each other into their nineties. The topic between them then was who would live longest. Ellie died at 96, Mary Angela at 97.

Aged 20, she decided to become an Ursuline, and joined the community at Forest Gate. She made her Novitiate at Haacht in Belgium and joined the Forest Gate Community in 1901.

The community had now been at Forest Gate for over 30 years and much had changed in that time. The sparsely populated Upton village that the first founding sisters met, was now a densely populated urban area. As early as 1879 Mother Xavier Hynes, a former boarder, discerned the need for a Grammar Day School in this rapidly developing area, and opened St Angela's with 12 pupils. When she retired there were 700 on roll. The General inspection report describes Mother Xavier as "an able teacher of wide views and sympathies, who has deservedly gained the confidence of parents and girls."

It will come as no surprise that she quickly spotted Mary Angela's potential and counselled her as her successor. Subsequently in 1921 she became head of St

Angela's. It wasn't the easiest of beginnings. The Cardinal at the time, Cardinal Bourne, was very anxious that Catholic schools should be staffed by well-qualified teachers and had encouraged convents to send nuns to university. Mary Angela was currently in her final year studying for a French degree at Bedford College and living at the Mercy Convent in Marylebone. Unexpectedly Mother Xavier became seriously ill and Mary Angela had to manage St Angela's remotely whilst doing her French finals. Quite an achievement.

She continued as Headteacher at St Angela's until 1935. These years were probably her most fulfilled, offering scope to her educator's instincts, her creativity and her energy. She campaigned fearlessly so that the school received every penny and status to which it was entitled. In 1927 the General inspection report described the achievement since her appointment "marvellous, its value as impossible to estimate too highly." Whirlwind as she was, she nonetheless could enter whole-heartedly into the simpler things of life. On Fair Day 1925 someone had donated a puppy for the big raffle. She drew the winning ticket and announced "number 106 – Mother Angela Mary!" The puppy was duly presented to her and became a regular companion around school and featured in all subsequent staff photos.

In 1937 she became the third Provincial of the Roman Union and moved to Westgate. The province after 14 years was now well established and Westgate its centre and hub. Her first aim was to build a chapel worthy of the province.

It was designed by Mr Henry Horn and Sister John Stahl and built by Rooffs' builders who Mary Angela had known at Forest Gate. It remains an outstanding feature of the site. Mr Horn always kept a photo of it in pride of place in his office.

Whatever her mandate, her role was likely to be a lively, active and enterprising one. 1937- 1946 was destined to be a period like no other. In our section Ursulines 1923 – Vatican II we have seen the lead role she played in adapting Ursuline schools to the Butler 1944 Education Act.

The war years 1939 – 1945 presented unprecedented challenges. She herself was evacuated with the Westgate School and community to Wallingford in Oxfordshire. The London Houses, for which she now had overall responsibility, found themselves in ill prepared locations and often faced with insoluble dilemmas. **St Angela's** in the villages around Woodbridge in Suffolk, then at Thetford and finally at Newquay. **Ilford** at Ipswich and then Devizes, **Becontree** at Oxford and later at Littlemore, **Greenwich** at Hastings and then Brecon in South Wales. At this time in each London house a skeleton community remained of the elderly and those who cared for them. Stories abound to this day of the impossible problems of the evacuated nuns now managing billeted boarding schools often with no local classroom space allocated and the equally impossible demands of the provincial that religious life should continue with perfect regularity! But while she chastised and demanded regularity there was no doubting her fundamental sympathy, as she waged her own plan of invasion penetrating County Hall, the Ministry of Health, the Board of Education and Archbishop's House at Westminster to lodge her complaints about evacuation.

Every week or so a letter went out, addressed to " my very dear children at home and abroad", or "evacuated or otherwise". In them, she gave all the news, "in case you have not heard" about each convent, each group of evacuees, and when she was able to do so, about the Ursuline convents in Europe, caught up in the horrors of war. Whatever the location she arranged regular annual visitations to those evacuated and those at home. Provincial council meetings took place as regularly as ever. In 1946 the war and her provincial mandate ended and she settled briefly at Westgate.

She was by now in her late 60's and remained a natural leader and an experienced negotiator, able to put these skills into practice in the newly created governing bodies in our post 1944 schools. She also continued to be an active member of The Convent Schools Association, a progressive development that she, along with other well-established congregations, had been instrumental in setting up in 1928. In 1947 she returned to Forest Gate to organise the Metropolitan branch of this organisation.

For most of the information above I am indebted to Mother Winefride Sturman who wrote a brief life of Mary Angela at her death in 1976, but this leaves untouched her elder "stateswoman" years at the House of Studies at Parkside 1956- 1970 when the generation responsible for this book knew her. By this stage, her firebrand days were over with just the odd traces of exactitude remaining. "She's on the phone", a no-no that invariably provoked, "I hope she is comfortable!" But for most of us, she was a spirited, intelligent and lively woman, whom one felt privileged to have encountered. Here are a few memories and tributes from our Juniorate days.

"I used to love her lessons, because she relished what she was teaching, and always enjoyed the "juicy" bits of Latin literature, especially Livy! She had a very human understanding of dramatic works, especially Racine, Corneille and Moliere, and she knew how to convey her understanding of the characters in what could be considered as old and dusty dramas from the 17th century."

"She had a gift for making literature, philosophy and history come alive. I still remember her lessons on Plato's Republic. And of course, she always had her foot warmer under the table- Blarney by name!"

"She sharpened my mind! She introduced us to Plato's Republic. I'd never been so challenged and fascinated before by a book's arguments and style. Today I remember best "The Allegory of The Cave." The disappointment of the philosopher, when most people remained more comfortable living in mere shadows, rejecting a higher intellectual life. It pained me too!"

"All my life I had been educated in a convent school, but my formal reception into the Catholic Church was not until 1952, as a sixth-former at St. Angela's. The required instruction was taken care of by Mother Mary Angela Boord. I remember her quiet voice and firm convictions. I listened dutifully, feeling at ease but not always in agreement. Did I not, for example, find ballet an indecent form of entertainment?"

"Later, at the end of my year at Parkside, I was more in tune with her wisdom and insight. Her last piece of advice, well-nigh a command, was delivered at the front door as I was about to depart. I was not to allow 'them' to send me to another French convent to hone my language skills. Waste of time, in her opinion. No, I should insist on staying in a family. In 1960… a Junior insisting? … nun in *a family*? In this, as in so much else, Mother Mary Angela was far ahead of her time!"

Sister Peter Buck- Greenwich War Account

By August 1939, it was clear that war was imminent. Staff and children were recalled from their summer holidays and assembled at school each day with the stipulated hand luggage, ready to leave at short notice for an unknown destination. The summons to evacuate on September 1st arrived on 30th August. Early in the morning coaches assembled on Blackheath. The party comprised of 200 children with younger brothers and sisters and sixteen members of staff. Eight sisters and eight secular mistresses. Amid the ordinary bustle of New Cross station, with trains arriving and departing in quick succession, a very long train drew in on a separate platform on which St Ursula's waited with several other schools. The destination was guessed as Hastings quite quickly. The school remained in Hastings until 23rd June 1940 when they were moved to Brecon. What of Greenwich at this time? The 'phoney war' ended in June 1940 and in September the Battle of Britain was waged. **Sr Peter Buck,** who lived through it all at Greenwich describes her experiences.

"I returned from evacuation to help Mother St Victor with the school at Greenwich, which unofficially began to operate again. The older girls who wanted to take their public exams became the nucleus of the school. The first excitement was an incendiary bomb on the convent roof, just near the chapel and a blazing spitfire which lay outside the school gates. Until this time, we had no provisions for a shelter- the children's cloakrooms were set up with beds and later we moved to the kitchen corridor. One night in late September, like a bolt from the blue came a terrific crash, then silence. A land mine had exploded outside Ranger's Lodge. The structure of Hyde Cliff building was severely shaken, the roof was lifted, doors hung drunkenly off their hinges and windows were blown out. About a month later a high explosive bomb took off the corner of Hyde Cliff wing. The nuns were in the shelter at the time, which filled with gas and clouds of dust. What a picture of destruction the following morning! One classroom had been blown away along with one third of the big dormitory. Two big water tanks had been hit and emptied their contents down through the house. The damage was made worse by the exposure to the heavy rain which brought down ceilings, spoiling floors and walls. Throughout the winter months we were under constant bombardment. A good night's rest was impossible but no one was downhearted. Sr Anthony Dunbar with true British fidelity, loudly proclaimed "St George slay the dragon!"

On the feast of St Joseph, 19th March 1941 at 8pm, a Molotov Bread Basket fell on the convent. The fires spread rapidly and the convent was completely ablaze. With wet handkerchiefs around our faces we tried to salvage bedding, we raced with anything procurable and dumped it in the chapel. Water was not available until 3am due to the high demand in the area, but an hour later the fires were under control. Fr McKenna came to celebrate Mass at 5am and the light of the fire shone through the chapel windows giving a lurid glow. The children arrived as usual for school, some stayed to help but all were given two days' absence. Only the walls of 70 Crooms Hill were now standing. The contents of its four floors lay in a charred and smouldering mass within.

Gradually the raids grew less frequent and by May had ceased completely. Life for the next year was almost normal. By July 1942 almost all were home from Brecon, when suddenly in August fury broke out again. I was in the first room over the chapel taking a Plain Song practice when I saw a plane at eye level coming across the heath. It seemed to be coming straight for us, and machine gun fire could be heard. The girls dived under their desks but I was stunned and stared helplessly at the oncoming plane. The pilot was visible; he swept over our roof, passed between the convent and library straight for the town hall where he shot off the clock hands. He then dropped two bombs on the Naval College and bombed a local school as the children were going home. Casualties were high and two of our past pupils were killed.

Raids continued intermittently by day and night for the next two years. In June 1944 the doodlebugs started and one exploded in King George Street at the bottom of our gardens. From that time onwards, there was incessant dread from the flying bombs and pupil numbers in school dropped radically. The sixty girls who attended were all taking their public examinations and on many occasions, had to dive under their desks for protection. Nevertheless, the results were good. Much to everyone's relief, school finished on 16th July and on the afternoon of 27th July a siren sounded. We paid little attention to it and joined the other sisters in the lime-tree walk. The unmistakable sound of a doodlebug suddenly stopped and we knew it was meant for us. Some stayed where they were, others tried to protect themselves against benches and some fled towards the house. The flying bomb in its descent had tipped the elm tree outside the school gate and exploded there, uprooting the tree. The shell of the bomb flew through the parlour window where it poised itself on the table and caused a fire. The caretaker's cottage and most of the front part of the school was destroyed.

Our ordeal was nearing its end and the Ministry of Education granted us repair damage. On 6th January 1945 we were invaded by an army of 98 workmen, who with devoted skill and labour restored the school to order. Among them was a young Irishman who confided in Sr Colomba that he wanted to become a priest and Sr Agnes Curtin coached him in Latin O-Level so that he would be able to enter the seminary. He became the centre of the community's prayers. The last of the rockets came at the end of March and finally peace on 7th May 1945. It was blissful to be able to sleep at night and above all, to feel that the children could travel in safety and learn peacefully".

The Sisters surveying the damage to the roof

Sister Mary Carmel Pearce entered in 1954 to go to the missions. This very specific request went unnoticed by the powers that be but not by Mary Carmel who held her ground and in August 1959 left Heathrow - at that time it had one runway - for the Caribbean mission! She had no expectation of ever returning and gave herself heart and soul to this new life, which was very fulfilling for her and for the province where she remained for over 50 years serving as provincial for two separate stints!

As with many well-laid plans, God had other ideas and she decided to return to England when her only sister became ill and required care. With 50 years of totally differing experiences it was often difficult to find common ground for the stories that make up the warp and woof (fabric) of daily chat. However, she had an incredible memory of her wartime childhood and her early schooling, which she was able to share, just at the time when there was a revival of interest, in an event that was rapidly becoming history. Wartime brought many changes, challenges and new ideas to Ursuline life and this seems an appropriate place to include war as seen through the eyes of a child.

Jean attended St Vincent's school Becontree where she had been a pupil for 2 terms. Becontree was near Dagenham Dock so an area due for evacuation. Her mother was one of the volunteer helpers in this new venture. So, on the finally disclosed

September date she, together with her 5 and 12-year-old daughters, arrived at a station to take the train to a still unknown destination, where they were met by the Women's Voluntary Service (WVS) to be allocated to a new home.

Jean remembers being miserable and tearful, which didn't enhance their chances, as prospective hosts made their choices. Their mother wasn't happy either and decided they would all go back home and face life together with their father, even if it meant being bombed. So, her war years were spent in blitz ridden London. She remembers being able to spot planes in the sky, having her own stash of shrapnel, and sharing the concern of the local women when a young German lad was shot down in his plane; no doubt evoking in the women visions of similar horrors for their own sons and husbands.

Her father, who faked his age to join up in the 14-18 war, was too old for this one but was active in the Home Guard. Being so near Dagenham, this was a dangerous, heartrending and busy job especially during the London blitz. Their own house was badly damaged, her father lost all the birds in his beloved aviary, a loss painful enough to reduce him to tears.

Education too suffered. When they first returned to schooling, lessons took place in the front room of their council house, her mother popping in frequently to offer yet another cup of tea. When the majority of pupils had trickled back and St Vincent's re-opened, lessons were often held in a room under the church and they learned to dive under their desks when Doodlebugs made their daytime appearances. By this time six years had passed and Jean was now 11 and in the scholarship year she remembers an "under the desk dive" during the actual exam and a return to task after the "all clear." She was lucky in the result and joined St Angela's that September.

These were hazardous and difficult times no one would wish to repeat, but for a young person growing up, this was home, where despite everything it was where you were loved and a good place to be.

Sister Mary Carmel died on the 16th March 2023.

Mother Magdalen Bellasis

Born in Dalhousie, Northern India in 1891 the family came to England when she was young to arrange for her education and that of her brother Eric. Her last year of schooling was at the Cheltenham Ladies' College, and soon after that, she became a Catholic.

After leaving school, she obtained a high position in the civil service and in the New Year's Honours List of 1918, she had the distinction of being one of the first to receive the new award of the M.B.E from King George V, for her services in one of the War Ministries during the First World War.

In 1919 she entered the Ursuline Community of Angers which at the time was living in exile in Cheltenham. When the community returned to France in 1931 and Fulwood was closed, four English sisters remained. Sr Magdalen was among them and became headmistress at the Ursuline School in Thornton Heath. In 1932 she became novice mistress at Westgate, until being sent to Rome for her tertianship in 1934. She remained in Rome until 1945 where she was Prioress of the Generalate community. It was during the war years in Rome that she wrote her diary. It is impossible to include all the stories but below are a few extracts which enable us to understand what it was like living in Rome at the time.

Her first entry was made in **June 1940**
'The telephone between The Vatican City and Rome has been cut off. But coming and going is freely allowed. No-one asks your business or demands to see your passport. We had a message from the Papal Nuncio here saying that no religious would be interfered with on account of the war. The interests of all nuns of 'enemy' nationality have been placed in his hands by the Italian government…During the night the sirens sounded. I thought a practice had been announced and took no notice, but some people got up. I think it is absurd to think the allies will bombard Rome.'

Tuesday, August 27th 1940
"We had occasion to go into the Basilica of St Agnes, which is our parish church and found the mosaic of the apse entirely covered in tinfoil. The sacristan told us it was aluminium, a protection against possible damage during air raids. Aeroplanes very busy and fussy, flying low over the houses. A story says that one of our air raid warnings was due to Mussolini looking out of his window one night and seeing a number of lights showing. He immediately rang up anti-aircraft headquarters and said "Have the sirens sounded to give them a fright!"'

Thursday, October 10th 1940
'Great joy- another letter from home! It seemed an endless time since the last ... .How glad I am that we took the precaution last year of arranging a code for our letters in case of war. We can say a good deal more than would be allowed in plain language.'

Sunday, October 13th 1940
'The general opinion pretty well everywhere seems to be that the Germans may as well admit that their plan has failed as regards to England...It is certainly true that London's resistance to air attack has amazed everyone...Mussolini has made a speech with unfriendly allusions to the Holy Father. That is a bad omen.'

Sunday, November 24th 1940- Papal Mass
'It was to be a penitential function and not a festivity. He had neither Sedia Gestatoria nor trumpets...We heard his homily which was very moving. He recalled how he had done all, absolutely all, in his power to avert war, but no one would listen to him. Now he could but turn to heaven and pray for mercy on his children...Those who were there said it was most beautiful. The crowd was so silent, no talking or jostling; they really had gone there to pray.'

Tuesday, March 4th 1941
'We are trying to buy a cow! Milk, butter and cheese are falling off all at once and with the diminution of meat it makes a problem, not so much for those in good health but for delicate members of the household and they are fairly numerous.'

April, 1941
'A visitor told us the latest motto being repeated in Rome: "if the English win the war, we shall lose. If the Germans win, we are lost".'

Monday, September 15th 1941
'The Germans in Rome have been buying up everything in the shop to such an extent that an order has gone out that no foreigners may buy in any shop above the value of 20 lire'.

Monday, September 22nd 1941
'...A girl we know told us that in the street where she lives, the news went around that a certain shop had some potatoes. She ran there at once...but there was such pushing and clamouring that the shop woman was desperate and reduced to tears. "You must give me time to weigh them" she protested...discontent is constantly growing."

Friday, November 28th 1941
'The telephone man has been here on some pretext and when he had finished pottering about we found that he had fixed a second wire to our receivers...we found a new wire running along the corridor...now the Gestapo can listen not

only to what is said on the telephone but to all that is said near it. We shall have to put up notices…Taci!' *(shut up)*

There is a gap in the diary between February 1942 and July 1943. The reason given is that Sr Magdalen had sent her diary to England but it never got there, discouraging her to write until 1943 when events started to move closer to her.

Thursday, July 22nd 1943
'We only have four inches of water left in our reservoir and it is tepid and disagreeable to drink. We have begun sending out for drinking water to a public fountain.'

Monday, July 26th 1943
'This morning we were greeted with much more unexpected news: a veritable thunderbolt…the gardener came up to me and said "Mother, they've sent away Mussolini because he has ruined the country". Anti-fascist manifestations were everywhere…the fascist emblems were torn down, fascist badges snatched off people and a bonfire of black shirts was made.'

Saturday, August 14th 1943
'They say Milan cathedral was hit last night. I am sorry. I simply cannot understand people who say "Well Westminster Abbey was hit", as if that ended the matter. Because one beautiful thing is damaged another may as well be damaged too. It is not my idea of logic.'

One 3rd September 1943, an armistice was signed between the Kingdom of Italy and the allies.

Friday, September 17th 1943
'A young Jewish girl whose parents had been deported to Germany came and asked us to take her in with her little sister of eight. They escaped from somewhere in Croatia and got into Italy as best they could. The child was dressed as a boy and brought by a lady who had a little son mentioned on her passport. Poor things: what a childhood!'

Saturday, September 18th 1943
'My last Russian Jewish convert came around very agitated, saying that the Germans were beginning to hunt out Jews again and wanted to hide. I said I was afraid that she would not be safe with us, as we are under surveillance…She asked if the lunatic asylum next door would take her in if she paid…I thought they would not take her without a certificate.'

Monday, September 20th 1943
'We have become accustomed to the rifle shots that we hear every night that we pay no attention to them…However, today one of our Mothers…found a hole in one of the windows panes and a piece of wood splintered off the shutter and a bullet in a glass-topped box the other side of the

room. We shall put the bullet in our war museum…It shows that it is better not to loiter at the window.'

In September 1943, the Germans were rounding up all the men they could get hold of. Dragging them off buses and out of shops and cars to be sent to fight. Sr Magdalen makes reference to ten 'hiding' within the convent. Their gatekeeper, gardener, their sons and several others.

Monday, October 18th 1943
'In the evening one of our temporary guests came to us in tears, saying her aunt and uncle and all their children (Jews) had been carried off by the Germans. They say they are put into cattle trucks and taken no one knows where. Day after day people come begging to be taken in and hidden from the Germans. If only Rome could be relieved soon, what a lot of misery would be spared.'

Wednesday, December 22nd 1943
'…A telephone message from some unknown person to our other house told them to expect a visit of inspection. *(The Gestapo were searching convents looking for Jews)* We told our temporary guests who all decided to spend the day elsewhere. By 10am all had gone and we were busy making their rooms look unoccupied…It proved a false alarm and they drifted back one by one.'

Wednesday, February 10th 1944
"I had to go to the Vatican on business and met an escaped British officer. He is a sapper and was taken prisoner in Libya having been left behind to blow up a bridge. He was taken to Italy but escaped…The police have visited our other house to inquire whether it was illegally sheltering Jews or other wanted persons. The Italian was extremely discreet and polite but said "You may very likely have a visit before long from the Germans and they will not be so discreet as we are, so be prudent".'

In 1943 there is a sense of the war intensifying around Rome, Sr Magdalen comments that she feels they are a step closer to the end of war as they go from rattling windows to broken windows. There is a constant mention of bombardments, food and water shortages, the death of the fowls from disease and the theft of their cow. Morale increases with the news of the allied advance towards Rome but is crushed within a few days with news of German success. A common phrase is "If only the allies could get here quicker".

Wednesday, March 8th 1944
'Rations are beginning to diminish perceptibly: though what we have is still enough for most of us, it is not really enough for the Sisters who have done a hard day's work in the wash house or garden. We have nothing left in the kitchen garden but cabbages.

Thursday, March 23rd 1944 'A priest from Brescia called on our Italian Mother to give news of our house there. A part of the Fascist government has gone there and they have begun to arrest the leading Catholics- priests or laymen who are not afraid of saying what they think. Some have already been shot. This one escaped.'

Monday, June 5th 1944

'The Americans have arrived! The Germans are gone!...The roads were soon full of people coming out of their hiding places. There were great demonstrations of joy, especially in St Peter's, where they shouted for the Holy Father and applauded him frantically...An extraordinary quiet reigns now.'

Tuesday, June 6th 1944

'At midday the great news was of the landing in the N. of France, but no details.'

The bread rations increased by 50% and food was distributed to British subjects. On showing three British passports, Sr Magdalen and another sister were given three kilos of flour.
There are only a few more entries in the diary and they are spread across four months. There is only one entry in August which speaks about the lack of food but high morale as they hope for a speedy end to the war. The diary ends on Sunday September 10th 1944.

Sr Magdalen returned to England in 1945 where she was Provincial until 1952. In 1955 she was elected Secretary General of the Order and from 1959-1965 she was the Assistant General. From 1954-1962 she was the first Vice Principal of the newly opened Pontifical Institute in Rome, Regina Mundi. For her services she was awarded the pontifical medal 'Pro Ecclesia et Pontifice'.

On her return to England, Sr Magdalen acted for a short time as Prioress Delegate of the community of Christ's College, Liverpool. From Liverpool she moved to Westgate-On-Sea where she spent her remaining years. In spite of growing infirmity, she continued to work ceaselessly, translating articles and books, teaching English to foreign students, looking after the community library and keeping up her correspondence all over the world until the day before she died. She was remembered for being a dedicated Ursuline with rare precision, great integrity, selflessness and a beautiful smile.

Sister John Stahl

Sister John combined being a Novice Mistress with a missionary career, with a significant difference! Her 30 year stint as Novice Mistress began in 1939. She was evacuated with the Ilford school to Devizes when she learned of her appointment. The novitiate too, along with Westgate boarding school was evacuated to tranquil Wallingford-on-Thames and remained there throughout the war. The buildings at Westgate being commandeered by the Women's Auxiliary Air Force (WAAF). At the end of the war Novices and students returned to Westgate only to find that neither school nor novitiate under WAAF hands were quite as they had left them!

There are no sisters alive today who can remember a novitiate before 1939. During her thirty year span Sr John Stahl met many changes from Latin to English in the Mass, walled convents to suburban houses. It was her design of a revised habit that won General Chapter approval in the 1960's. Clearly not designed by Dior, it did have the advantage of being easily modified and is still the basis of the habit worn in many provinces. The similar training that so many of us experienced has given us a common grounding and enabled a good province bonding as well as giving us a fund of anecdotes and stories to share!

When Sister John retired she still had many resources to draw on. She volunteered for the Missions and went to Botswana, a relatively new Ursuline development, where she found a new lease of life and many openings for her artistic skills. She spent many happy years there, before returning to Shotton to be near her sister. There she became involved in Parish life.

There are two facts that every one of her novices would remember. She was dog phobic and sun phobic, but somehow these phobias managed to disappear in Botswana, which had both dogs and sun in abundance. Here we see her in Botswana with Queen Elizabeth II and a woman's group.

"Have engraved on your mind and heart all your dear daughters"
-St Angela Merici

Sister Pia Gombos

Sr Pia, Maria Gombos, was born in a little village near Gyor in Hungary. She remained all her life deeply attached to her homeland, though destined from early youth to live always in exile. Her family lived a little distance from Gyor and as a young girl, Pia was sent to the Ursuline convent in the town centre for her schooling. This was a substantial foundation in the continental style, a spacious property with a large community, and a prestigious school established to educate the daughters of the middle class.

Her mother's sister had entered the community at an earlier time, but died at a very young age, and her tomb is still to be seen in the convent burial vault. Pia went as a boarder, and then, she in her turn, entered the community, just before the second world war in 1939. She took a degree in Physics at the university, but although she showed considerable promise, her formal teaching career in the classroom was short-lived.

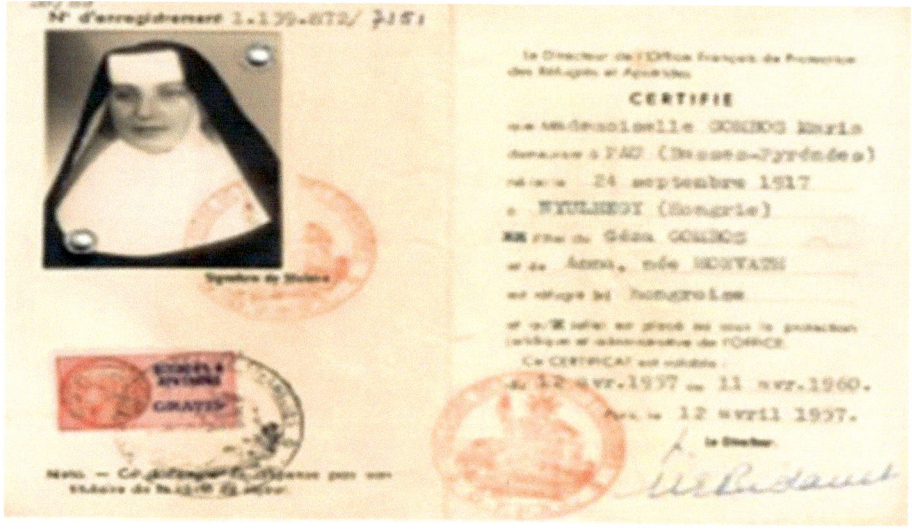

At the end of the war in 1945, Hungary, as an ally of Germany, was overrun by Russian troops and the border to the west was sealed. The convents were closed and religious practice became illegal. A group of young sisters, Pia among them, managed at this critical point to escape from the country and find their way to France. Here, Pia officially classed as a refugee, joined the community at Pau, a little town at the foot of the Pyrenees. She arrived in 1947 and was to live there for the next 15 years.

At that period, less urgency was attached to mastering a new language and Pia was not an ardent linguist. She learnt French and much later English – she was even to pass the written English exams offered by Pitman's at elementary and intermediate level.

Then in 1956 came the Hungarian Rising – the valiant attempt by her fellow countrymen to wrestle back their freedom from the ever-harsher domination of the Russians. The border to the west opened briefly and floods of refugees poured out. A considerable number found their way to England and settled in the London area. It took a while for them to find housing and employment, but as they settled they needed a focus for their cultural identity and this came to centre on Mindzenty House, west of Hammersmith. Here, they looked for support and encouragement. Pia was far away in Pau, until one day - out of a clear blue sky - she was asked to come to London to help them. It was 1962 and it proved to be her true calling.

Language was no longer a barrier and in this Hungarian setting she came into her own. For over 35 years this was her life, travelling purposefully across London, wherever she was needed and in all weathers, regularly to Mindzenty House in the West but also out to Essex or over to Croydon, leaving the convent at Greenwich early in the day and returning late in the evening. Sr Pia organised her days quietly and unobtrusively, so that few people had much idea of her undertakings.

But among her people, her personality blossomed. She was a valued teacher, an inventive organiser, artistic and creative. More than that, she was warmhearted and sympathetic, joyous and companionable. She kept alive the traditions of her country and gave the exiles a sense of home in an alien environment. A number found their way to Greenwich to visit her, and the highlight of the year was always the feast of St Nicolas, a special celebration for the English-born children of these Hungarian parents.

As the years went by, the original refugees encountered the difficulties of ageing. Pia remained faithful to them, developing an extensive telephone apostolate and visiting them in their homes. Restrictions on travelling to Hungary also eased and she was able to meet up with her sister and become acquainted with the younger generations of her family. She loved to be at the centre of Hungarian pilgrimages - to Fatima, to Rome, to Cardinal Mindzenty's tomb and always her prayers were in Hungarian. She had a little black prayer book always at hand, with her favourite devotions, a picture of the miraculous Virgin in the church at Gyor, and a constant range of Hungarian literature, filled with the life of the church.

Every evening she tuned in to Vatican Radio for the Rosary in Hungarian and remained constantly alert for news of her people and their fortunes. She became naturalised as a British citizen in 1970. This removed the ambiguity of being a refugee, but at heart nothing changed. She was always Hungarian.

On her death, she willed that her ashes be taken back to belong once more to her native country.

Sister Kwyrina Karas

In May 1936, Sr Kwyrina entered the Ursuline Postulate in Lwow, Poland. Much to her family's grief, she was sent to finish her Novitiate in England in 1938. When Germany invaded Poland in 1939, she lost contact with her family and never knew of their fate. She did not know that they had been transported to a labour camp in Siberia. Her brother Dr Adam Karas writes about his experiences and the moment he was finally reunited with his sister. Below is an extract taken from an article in the Catholic Herald.

"We were awakened at 3am by Russian soldiers. They said there was going to be a tremendous amount of fighting going on in the region. Once we were assembled in the railway yard it was evident we were not being evacuated for our own protection, but as prisoners of war for labour camps in Siberia. They packed us on to cattle cars, about 60 people to a car with no toilets, nothing. We travelled for almost six weeks before we finally arrived at our destination.

Everyone over 11 was put to work building railway tracks through Siberia. In return, people were given food. The amount of food was in proportion to the work you completed. We would secretly pray to Jesus; we would gather together and the whole family would pray. We were often caught and badly beaten as this was not allowed. The combination of cold weather and hunger led to sickness and death. Survivors envied the dead. Our first tragedy as a family was the death of our sister Angela, who died giving birth to a girl. Eighteen months later the girl died of starvation. After her burial, her grave was pillaged and the sheet she was wrapped in was gone. Despite the death of her daughter and granddaughter, my mother would never let us fall into despair, she would continue rallying us. She kept telling us that whatever it is, trust in God and eventually we'll come out of it alright. After two years we were sent to Khirghistan in the south of Russia. A milder climate but greater starvation.

In 1943, bowing to the pressure of their British and American allies, Russia began to release Polish prisoners. Many Polish men quickly joined the armed forces, including my two brothers. After we were released we were shipped to Iran which was supposed to be the beginning of a new life. Instead, it was the end for many. We were given a good meal, which probably killed more people than anything else. We were totally on a fasting stomach and they gave us fatty foods. That's what killed my mother three days later.

Meanwhile, the governments of Mexico, Argentina, Africa and India were willing to take a quota of Polish refugees. We wanted to go to Mexico or Argentina as these were close to the United States, but we were sent to India where we spent five years in a camp near Kolhapur."

After WWII, four of the children moved to England with their older brothers who had joined the armed forces in 1943. As the years passed, the siblings went their separate ways. Three lived in England, two in the United States, one in Canada and one in Australia. Although they had seen each other here and there, they had not all been together at the same time in 48 years.

In 1984 the seven surviving members of the Karas family came from four different countries to reunite in London. They sang together, they stayed together, they ate together, they toured London together- but most important, they were together for the first time in 48 years. All seven reminisce about how their mother's spirit continues to strengthen their lives. Adam Karas said "I have trust in her spirit as a mother. She has a great influence in my life and I constantly call on her for help. Mother's Day is like a feast day for us, because our mother lived the life of a saint."

The following is an extract of a speech given by Sr Kwyrina's sister Stefany at her Golden Jubilee celebrations in 1989.

"Sr Kwyrina, as our eldest sister, after the death of our brother Walenty, became our spiritual parent, we did not feel so alone, especially as the Ursuline Community became our extended family…she gave us consolation, inspiration, advice and above all unstinted love and care in times of trials. 'Hotline to God' as we fondly call her. I was recently the recipient of her care, not to mention the poor people in Poland. I have seen one room in the convent full of articles in it and was told that this room was called the 'Polish Embassy' by the other sisters. I should also imagine that if she was to put all the rosaries together that she makes for the missions, she could probably reach heaven."

Sister Brendan O'Riordan

She was one of six children born in Kerry. In 1944 she travelled to England and entered the Ursuline Convent in Westgate, along with her two sisters Donna and Maureen. She lived in Greenwich during her temporary vows and then gave devoted service to the community at Forest Gate. Later she went to the convent at Chester, which was her first and happy experience of living in the North West.

In the late 60's another venture lay before her: she was appointed to the Christ's College Community in Liverpool as cook. This was a different style of community life and as ever, she adapted to it perfectly. As well as nourishing the community, she transformed the backyard into a kitchen garden, she used it as an area open to all-comers: men of the road in need of sustenance or washing facilities (including one embarrassing incident where a bucket of water was taken for a full-scale bathtub!) to aspiring seminarians wanting counsel, encouragement and spiritual direction.

When Sr Brendan moved to Shotton in 1987, she quickly became familiar on the streets and in the lanes and alleyways. She was a woman born for friendship, no one passed without her offering a word of greeting, a touch of humour or a listening ear to their troubles. Blessed with a deep wisdom and humility, she saw life whole and enjoyed it. Peals of laughter could always be heard in any meeting or room she was in. A natural mimic, she also had a fund of funny stories and encouraging snippets, so her visits to the housebound and elderly were more than welcome. So many people would share their troubles with Sr Brendan that she did not plan her days as it stopped her from being free to listen to whoever called in. She walked miles to visit those she cared about, how open and welcoming her hands were to those in anxiety or distress or simply in need of food or drink. Her smile, gentle humour and the quiet God-based wisdom she possessed helped to console, cheer and encourage all whom she met.

Her popularity and the warmth people felt for Sr Brendan was clear to see from her funeral which was held in Connah's Quay. It was attended by two bishops, the local councillor, local MP and local MEP, Ambulance workers from Deeside Day care hospital and representatives from Churches Together. There were several members of the travelling community who she did a lot of work with and of course many local friends, parishioners and her Ursuline family.

Sister Monica Roberts

Sr Monica worked as a Media Resources Officer, designing and producing learning materials for St Philip Howard Catholic Secondary School in Poplar where she worked. She cycled 40 miles a week to and from Greenwich, where she lived, to her school in Poplar. She was a very fit person! In the summer of 1988, she began to feel unwell- tiredness, a persistent cold, bruising and aches and pains. She was not concerned and thought a 'good holiday would put her right'. Whilst on holiday in Scotland with four other sisters, she was diagnosed with cancer. Below are extracts from a presentation Sr Monica gave to a conference on 'Spiritual and Ethical Issues in Cancer Care' in October 1990. They are her own words of her long and brave fight with her illness.

"I am eternally grateful for the way the Scottish doctor broke it to me. "The blood test results would seem to indicate that you've got treatable leukaemia". For me, I think my whole approach to my leukaemia was inspired by the way this doctor broke the news to me. The inclusion of that one word "treatable" can, I believe, make all the difference…Two days later I was admitted into the Royal Marsden Hospital at Sutton, Surrey.

Going into hospital was all so new and bewildering, but the nurses and doctors were very sympathetic and understanding and took the time and trouble, then and always, to explain things over and over again to me. Every person with cancer copes with their illness in their own way. Mine was to find out as much as I could about leukaemia…armed with knowledge, I felt I could fight it. From the onset I wanted to know the absolute truth…initial treatment and long term. General prognosis- a painful question to ask.

I had hoped that my initial stay in hospital might be 4-6 weeks but it turned out to be 4 months! I had a central line plumbed into me, bits of plastic sticking out of me and had a visit from the 'wig lady'. With her help and that of some friends, I chose a style and colour of wig that as near as possible matched my own hair.

In the main entrance hall of the hospital there is a beautiful statue of a mother and child. The inscription reads: "The mother and child is a symbol of love and confidence, protection, help and happiness, set here to express our purpose to welcome, comfort, relieve and cure" How magnificently everyone at the Royal Marsden lives up to that ideal. I am so grateful that I've experienced so much of all the inscription says.

I have been asked if I blame God, got angry with Him, blamed myself…I certainly don't blame God- or myself. No one wants to be ill. Illness, like many other things in life, comes uninvited, we simply have to go through the experience. I believe that there is a God; that we are not left to fate or chance. And I believe that God has a plan and a purpose for my life and every life that is essentially for our good, though we may not comprehend it. Apparently the most requested record on the hospital radio is Lena Martell's 'One day at a time' and the chorus of this became another prayer "One day at a time sweet Jesus, that's all I'm asking of you".

My initial chemotherapy passed off without too much nausea and vomiting but I did become weaker. After the first treatment, there was still evidence of cancer in my marrow and I would need a second round of chemotherapy. I was plunged into despair but knew I was in the right place."

Sr Monica became very ill, she picked up infections and required one to one nursing. She was taken to the high dependency unit where she was ventilated and a tracheotomy became necessary. When she woke from her sedation she had no recollection of this critical time and could not speak or move. After five weeks in the High Dependency Unit, she was able to return to her ward where she had to relearn how to stand, walk and communicate.

"I finally left hospital, just before Christmas and the next few months were very hard- a long, slow climb back to a basic level of fitness, both physically and mentally. Just before Easter '89 I asked a close friend to help me plan my funeral Mass, which I wanted to have ready, just in case!"

In April 1989, Sr Monica had an autograft. She gradually gained her strength and moved to the convent at Westgate-On-Sea and began working part time. She visited friends and relations in Dublin and spent some time in Dutch convents in the summer. In July she did a 58-mile sponsored cycle ride for the Royal Marsden and raised £1500. In September Sr Monica relapsed and developed severe infections.

"My experience of leukaemia has made me realise how very precious each new day is. In one sense every new day since my diagnosis has been a bonus…I have learned to live one day at a time and to live each day to the full…I believe people die when they are ready for God."

Sr Monica Roberts died on the 31st August 1991 of Leukaemia. She was 40 years of age and in her 14th year of religious life.

'What you are is God's gift to you, what you become is your gift to God'.

> "God has planted this Company, he will never abandon it"
> -St Angela Merici

Sister Timothy Pinner- Christ's College

Sr Timothy is today in South Africa and is here seen tutoring an A Level Student

Thinking about what to write in this reflection, there was one word which kept recurring – CHANGE!

When Christ's College of Education opened in Liverpool in 1964 with 200 first year men and women students it was a new venture for the Ursulines in England in conjunction with the secular clergy. Teacher education was expanding as more teachers were required and its qualification was *changing* from a two year certificate to a three year degree (validated by Liverpool University); Catholic Religious education in schools was *changing* as new syllabuses were introduced – I can remember the name of Fr Somerville; It was the era of the Vatican Two Council and things were beginning to *change* in the Church and Religious life. Sixteen years later, when the Ursulines withdrew from the College, it was still a time of *change* as three Christian colleges amalgamated to eventually form Hope University validating its own degrees in a wider range of subjects.

The first year at the College was a challenge and traumatic: some of us (two Ursuline sisters and two diocesan priests) had had a year of College experience at Strawberry Hill, Twickenham but even with this the teaching experience was different. We were working with young adults, helping them adapt to their new responsibilities for themselves, away from home; we were not only teaching our own subjects but also analysing and communicating how to teach them. The new College buildings were not complete – the main teaching block was still to be completed and the new convent. Teaching was arranged in common rooms and dining areas; a possibility because the full number of students was not yet complete. And the sisters lived in the small Sick Bay building. The staff was also small in number, to be increased over the years and we all assisted with tutorials for the General Divinity course, which all students followed and which prepared them for Religious teaching in schools. The trauma came at the end of the first term: it had become customary among the staff to say "after Christmas" as we then expected to have all the College buildings (not the convent!) completed and we could begin to develop our own subject areas. But in December Fr Louis Hanlon had a major car accident and died in early January: so "after Christmas" took on a much more serious meaning. Sister Benedict Davies took on full responsibility for the College for the rest of the year and the incident bonded together the first group of students in a manner which is difficult to fully explain.

In some ways the founding Ursuline community – of which I was a member throughout the Ursulines sixteen years at Liverpool - was also special: not only because of the bonding through the accident but also because of that first year when twelve of us lived in such close proximity in the small Sick Bay building. However, as for the College, these years were also a time of challenge and trauma for the Sisters. Religious Life was *changing* and we found ourselves moving into some of these *changes* perhaps more rapidly than others: our contact with the other staff was more direct both in the staffroom and in dining, as during the first year circumstances required that we take our midday meal in College; going out was freer as we all went individually to visit the school for which we were responsible on teaching practice – which meant, incidentally that we got to know very quickly the active Catholic atmosphere in the Liverpool Archdiocesan schools; our contact with students was more direct through the tutorial system; and last, but not least, dress *changed* as new formats were introduced but also because of the needs of field work and camps! Our trauma, as a community, came more towards the end: some later members were not involved with the college apostolate but with the developing other works of that era – teaching in non-Ursuline schools, nursing, parish visiting etc… These *changes* also brought the inevitable tensions into community life.

This account has inevitably become not merely a reflection on Christ College but a personal look at my own Ursuline life. My years at Liverpool were very formative: I knew Liverpool well having visited my priest uncle there many times as a teenager – and in fact the College site was situated in his old parish! It became related to my development as an Ursuline educator, giving me a wider and deeper view of education in general and Mathematical education in particular which I have been able to carry into "Leading a new Life" in England, Cameroon and Southern Africa.

Father Hanlon, to the left of Bishop Beck was the first principal of Christ's and was instrumental in its foundation. He died tragically as a result of a car accident, he was in fact on his way to St Angela's Forest Gate to see their production "Noye's Fludde" when his car tyre blew. Unfortunately, he was only in post for three months. He was succeeded by Fr Doyle who was principal for many years, Sister Benedict was vice principal from the opening of the college until 1973. She was succeeded by Sister Mauren Coyne until 1980 when our community at Liverpool closed. Christs College lives on today as part of Hope University Liverpool.

Sr Timothy went to the missions when
Christs College closed. She worked in Cameroon and South Africa
She now lives in the Ursuline Convent in Krugersdorp, South Africa.

It will probably come as a surprise that as a Province we were so engaged in the London 2012 Olympics. There were two reasons for this. The Forest Gate community was within walking distance of the main Olympic site and in 1996 **Citizens UK**, a grassroots alliance of many local communities working together, took shape in the four East London Boroughs of Hackney Newham, Tower Hamlets and Walthamstow. It was then known as The **E**ast **L**ondon **C**ommunities **O**rganising (TELCO). Its Founder, Neil Jameson during his research period was funded from 3 principal sources, Brentwood RC Diocese, St Katharines' Foundation Limehous**e** and Cadbury Trust. From the outset it received warm support from many Catholic Parishes and groups and of our Ursuline Province.

By 2000 TELCO began to look seriously to England's Olympic possibilities. By this time, we had learned to work together across faiths and borough boundaries and people of no faith. We were also aware of the longstanding deprivation of the four boroughs in which we lived and that the Olympics could be a transforming influence.

In the subsequent weeks and years, London Citizens worked with communities and schools to ensure local involvement and flesh out the essentials of London's ethical bid. Our goals were: employment for local people, all jobs on the site (including subcontracted ones) to be paid at least the London Living wage, A Community Land Trust offering affordable housing in the Olympic Park and park and sporting venues to become a lasting legacy usable by local residents.

Our Ursuline community took an active interest and gave practical support throughout the long road. We put up posters in church and were backed up by support from the priests. So, our parish knew it was a local St Bonaventure's boy who was selected as one of the team of four to present the case to the international Olympic Committee. Later a St Angela's girl, who was also a parishioner, was selected to present the bid in Lucerne and be part of the borough team in Singapore. We took part too in the wild excitement in Trafalgar Square, when hope-against-all-hope, the vote was declared in England's favour.

Sister Catherine Kelly- Faith and the Olympics

More Than Gold is the Faith arm of the Olympics. Its dream is to enable thousands of churches to taste the excitement of reaching their community in fresh and on-going ways. Many churches and religious groups were involved in the London Olympics and Catholics played a significant part. The three Catholic churches closest to the stadium had large screens showing the events while at the same time offering tea, coffee and a listening ear. Franciscan friars from Italy, South America and England were available to talk to visitors. The Sion Community of Brentwood ran the *Joshua Camp*, a 12-day residential event centred at St Bonaventure's school Forest Gate.. About 150 young people aged 18 – 25 from many countries took part. They went out into the local community and difficult areas of London, such as Soho to perform acts of service, including inviting local young people to engage in sport, music and drama. A number of Olympians visited the camp.

Ursuline Involvement

Our community became involved with More than Gold after they made a presentation at the Leyton Orient Football ground in 2010 explaining all the areas in which they would be working. There would be street pastors, games pastors, chaplains and many areas of hospitality. These people would be available on the streets, at the airports and in the Olympic Park offering help. Once the Olympics began there was daily Mass in the Olympic village and many Bible study sessions. The chaplains were really impressed by the amount of religion shown by the competitors.

The director of More Than Gold also asked if anyone would be available for some voluntary office work. I offered my services and began work for one day a week in January 2011. For the first few months I was a general dog's body filling 5000 folders with 9 leaflets, answering the door etc. I even brought some boxes of the folders home so that Sr. Mary Charles was also able to be involved. One day I went into another office and found the Operations Director struggling with the finances and the Quick Books programme. I was explaining what he needed to do when he asked me to take over so I have helped with the finance from then on.

In every Olympics there is a scheme which offers free bed and breakfast accommodation to families of competitors who would find it difficult to afford hotel fees. In 2012 we welcomed the mother of a Canadian Olympian female boxer and her friend and in the Paralympics the wife of the Canadian blade runner. She herself had been a bronze medallist in the wheelchair event in Beijing.

Several sisters were able to attend events in both sets of games as affordable tickets were available to local residents. Sadly, for me this work came to an end during November. It was a very enriching time for me: I engaged with so many Christians from different church traditions – even to the 'Church run bar" in Soho, for those people looking for God but unable to go into a building called church!

Olympic Torch

Two of our Ursuline Communities outside London had direct links with the Olympic Torch as it made its way round England. Westgate School and Lourdes Nursing Home had a special visit and Sisters Vianney and Gwyn caught up with it in North Wales. We also had some American Ursuline students here working on an Ursuline Links Project who lined up on Romford Road Forest Gate to see it pass.

Westgate

As the Olympic torch wended its way through Kent, it stopped at the Ursuline College for over an hour. It was carried round the drive, lined with students to the Chapel lawn where the ceremony was held.

The theme of the ceremony was the 100 days of peace. We were reminded that all wars stopped for the duration of the Games in Ancient Greece. Isaiah's words 2:4 'They will

Sister Dolores Caine and Joan Moloney at the Torch Ceremony

hammer their swords into ploughshares and their spears into pruning hooks; nations will not lift up arms against nations, neither shall they learn war any more' were very significant. We were reminded that it is A Time to Shine through the Torch Relay.

The most potent symbol of the 100 days of peace was the release of five white doves, one at a time, by students as those present said: 'There is no peace without justice. Let it begin with me.' The ceremony ended with a blessing before the Torch continued on its way beyond Thanet.

Olympics at St Angela's

The Olympic Legacy of St Angela's is multi dimensional. The students of St Angela's Ursuline were privileged to take part in the run-up to the London 2012 Olympics. Student involvement ranged from attending events at the Aqua Centre to view diving; especially exciting was Tom Daley with his inward 1½ somersault pike, to the handball test and boxing test events.

Students were also invited to meet British Olympians including Linford Christie and Tessa Sanderson.

Our 6th Form students were successfully chosen to be part of the biggest show on earth at the opening and closing ceremonies; their auditions were led by an ex St Angela's girl and included routines being watched by Danny Boyle. Here are some of their comments:

"Where do I begin, my experience has been fantastic rehearsing in preparation for the ceremony has been absolutely amazing and so much fun. I've had the chance to work with great choreographers and meet new people; rehearsals are always enjoyable and I loved learning and perfecting all our routines. I'm so glad I took up the opportunity to participate in this big show and I wouldn't trade it in for anything it's been awesome".

"The whole experience has been unforgettable and worthwhile."

"So far the rehearsals are going great, the dance is coming along and it looks good. I'm so grateful to be there to take part. I can't wait for the show day!"

The St Angela's Gospel Choir were one of five choirs selected from almost 40 choirs to perform at the Sainsbury's School Games 2012 at the Olympic Park. They performed in front of the new Aquatics Centre and also at the Closing Ceremony in the Basketball Arena in front of 6,000 people. They sang five songs including 'The World's Greatest' by R Kelly and 'Rollin' in the Deep' by Adele. For the Closing Ceremony, they shared the same stage as Cover Drive, who later performed their hit singles 'Twilight' and 'Sparks'. Spellbound (Winners of Britain's Got Talent 2010) and Jonathan Edwards (world record holder in the triple jump) were also on stage.

Our school Sports Day in 2012 celebrated the athletes and cultures of the London 2012 Games, with each year group representing a continent and each form class a country. The five interlocking rings represent the five main regions brought together by the Olympic Movement: Africa, the Americas (North and South America combined), Asia, Europe and Oceania. As it says in the Olympic Charter, the five-ringed symbol "represents the union of the five continents and the meeting of athletes from throughout the world at the Olympic Games." The legacy of the games lives on in our students as they continue to live out the Olympic dream through their sporting prowess and the Ursuline Virtues.

Our Sports Day included a presentation to Shannen who designed the Olympic Mascot named Manderville and was presented by Tim Prendergast, a Paralympian.

During the Olympics themselves the school ran numerous trips to many events for the students of the school so that it was a real rather than discussed experience. To our huge excitement, Yasmin (Yr 8) and Sedji (6th former) were Olympic Torch Bearers!

Embracing Our Future

Discernment Beginnings

About ten years ago it was becoming very clear that we needed to do some concrete planning about the future. We began with a variety of questionnaires, but the one province meeting which made the difference was in the autumn of 2014. Sr. Maureen Moloney prepared an excellent presentation (later to be known as the "bedroom" PowerPoint) which gave us accurate information about our properties, numbers, ages and finances. It was soon very clear that some houses would need to close. We recognised that such closures would affect all of us in one way and another, but we felt we could not turn our backs on reality.

After further community and province discussions it was agreed that the provincial team would draw up an action plan. Over the Christmas period of 2014 people were wondering: will our house close?

Around this time a couple of us had attended a lecture given by Myriam Wijens, a Dutch theologian and professor of canon law, in which she spoke about the future of religious life. She referred us to an article written in 2012 entitled: Explorations on the "Completion" of Religious Institutes. Despite its title this was not a depressing read. It gave us the chance to evaluate and celebrate all the great work the Ursulines in England had been doing for more than 150 years. It also encouraged us to think creatively about the future.

Early in January 2015 members of the provincial team began the visits to the communities to tell them about the closures of communities. The hardest visits were to the communities in Lancaster, Shotton and Wythenshawe as the sisters there were asked to uproot themselves and move to the south of England in October 2015. While it would be wrong to minimise the pain this decision brought to the sisters and the people amongst whom they lived it must be said that, as true daughters of Angela, they were generous in their acceptance of the decision and showed great courage.

During all the community visits the sisters were clear that other closures would have to come in the next few years. The whole province was to walk this pathway together.

Discernment to Action

Sister Kathleen Colmer

"Our numbers were decreasing whilst our ages and personal needs were increasing; extra staff were being employed to assist us. Between 2015 and 2019 the sisters living in Wimbledon moved from their large house to a small flat close to Wimbledon station. The communities in Catford, Highmead (south-east London) and Ilford were closed; the sisters involved moved to other communities or to the Ursuline Care Home (Lourdes) at Westgate. Following refurbishment our house at Ilford was used for Youth activities organised by Ursuline Links.

During these years we sought help with the running of our Care Home, but each time we thought we had found a solution another problem arose. In addition, the numbers in the community at Westgate was decreasing. It was with heavy hearts that in 2018 we realised, once again, that hard decisions had to be made. It was felt that we needed to be closer together clustering around a London area. In late 2019, the Westgate community was closed; two years later, in September 2021, we closed Lourdes, our much-loved Care Home in Westgate. Our sisters from Lourdes are now happily living in Chestnut Manor Care Home, Wanstead.

In November 2023 the community at Greenwich will move to Ilford. Thus, the majority of the province will be living in close proximity to each other.

We have walked a challenging pathway together these past nine years. There has been pain, suffering, great courage and much faith shown along the way. As Minnie Louise Haskins wrote: "Go out into the darkness, and put your hand into the hand of God. That shall be to you better than light, and safer than a known way."

"Jesus Christ will be in your midst, he will enlighten and teach you what you have to do"
-St Angela Merici

Westgate Our 'HUB'

There is a rich history and many fond memories of the community at Westgate. As a place, it played a pivotal role in our history and our story. As stated, in September 2021 Lourdes Care Home was closed. It was a painful event for the Province but a necessary one. Now we look back and acknowledge with gratitude the part Westgate played in all our lives and dedicate this section to **Westgate- Our Hub.**

The Combes Law which suppressed all the religious teaching congregations in France, led to a sad and painful departure from Boulogne for the Ursuline Sisters in the August of 1904. As the sisters boarded their boat to Margate, a cry of 'Vivent les Soeurs" rang out from a group of former parents, pupils and friends who had come to say their goodbyes. A 22-year exile was to begin for this small group of French Ursulines- the founders of the Westgate convent. We owe much to those Sisters, but it is our living memories of Westgate that we focus on.

In 1926 the French Sisters returned to France and the Ursulines at Bideford took over the convent. In 1927, Dominic Tizard- the new Provincial moved the Provincialate from Crewe to Westgate. The Novitiate was also at Westgate, and this is where all our memories begin.

The School
From its foundation in 1904, the school has been the centre of the Westgate Community. It remained relatively small and homely, providing for an amazingly wide social and international mix of students and provided opportunities not available in our day schools. There were local scholarship girls, diplomats' daughters, Forces children, students from our missions seeking an English education, Local Authority children in care as well as families for whom a boarding education was

their natural choice. It was a happy place and provided a memorable education treasured for years. As one local authority boarder remembers "I loved Westgate, never before had I experienced a regular breakfast, lunch and dinner!". Westgate was a home and a school for many. For the sisters, juggling religious life, teaching and their boarding duties was difficult but rewarding. An amazingly large number of us, teachers and non-teachers, have worked there so it remains a very special place. Today as a day school and specialist Sports College it continues to provide the same high-quality education and care, sharing in our ongoing Ursuline Education Community projects.

The Novitiate

This is where "religious life" began for all of us. We each spent two years as novices in Westgate learning about the life to which we would formally and freely commit ourselves in three years' time (or 5 from 1958 onwards). The beautiful picture of the chapel lawn and garden above is embedded in most sisters' psyche as it was often our first encounter with our new and very different life.

In the novitiate, there were many new faces, titles, activities and rules to get used to. Our novice mistress Sister John Stahl, who had overall charge and retained the post for several years is very much part of "The Hub". She had a sub- novice mistress, who changed more frequently. Sr Anthony Murray who was a quiet, friendly, motherly character and someone you could talk to about normal things. She was followed by Sister Clare Tanter, one of Mother John Stahl's first novices, with a host of unofficial stories and a wonderful teacher of plainchant.

The grounds were beautiful, the fresh sea air and the vast space offered us a kind of freedom. We all have memories of picking blackcurrants, gooseberries and apples in the orchard, and of de-budding the chrysanthemums. But we also have memories of taking refuge in Calvary Walk, where we could face the challenges of- as the hymn says 'Our will and our wont days'.

Extensive grounds, a large orchard, together with the school and convent all required maintenance. Many people came to work for us and in those days a job was often for life and employees became like an extended family.

Province Centre

As a province centre, Westgate had three special features all to its advantage. It was near the sea, had spacious grounds and readily available accommodation. It was an

ideal place for holidays, recuperation, province meetings and was familiar to all of us. It was also the first port of call for visitors from other provinces.
We carry some fond memories of summer time activities. In the early fifties it hosted Jesuit run Cell Leadership courses for ages 18 to 25+. They were precursors of the Pope's world youth meetings of today.

Later there were Province joint retreats and conferences. Sister Antonia Ashpole recalls her experience. "One of the wonderful things that happened at Westgate was the beginning of 'Province Retreats'. These began in 1985 and there were five retreat givers, the whole Province was invited and we could choose which retreat director we wanted. I had eliminated four of the directors for reasons of my own and the only one left was the 'charismatic' retreat. I was half in and half out of the charismatic movement and I thought – I will do that one but the minute it starts 'Praise the lord, Alleluia' - I am off. And so, it began. The priest was a Holy Spirit Father (Cyril Byrne) and he started his first talk with 'Well, what are you expecting of this retreat?......the Holy Spirit is not pushy.... anything that is pushy is not the Holy Spirit!' I immediately started to relax and the whole retreat continued as if God was sitting there going through all the things that were bothering me - without me saying a word. It changed my life and I am so grateful for that Westgate retreat and to the priest who led the one I had."

In 1995 Sister Elizabeth and Sister Una began the English Language School at Westgate. It was the perfect place to host it; ample space and accommodation with seaside walks a stone's throw away. Ursuline Sisters came from other provinces abroad for a month to learn English. The Province played a vital role in the development of the English Language throughout the Roman Union.

All activities mentioned above, of course, fell heavily on the local community, who hopefully were marginally compensated by the slightly longer boarding school holidays,

Lourdes Care Home, founded in 1985

For many years sisters were cared for in sickness and old age within their own community with a sister as infirmarian and members of the community helping where necessary; this was our preferred option. But nursing became more specialised, sisters lived longer and there were fewer proportionately to care for them. We needed a rethink. Ideally it seemed better all round to group people together both for companionship and care. As with any change it took us a while to warm to the idea and as usual, the old seemed best. Westgate was the natural place to choose for this new community. It offered the opportunity of a beautiful garden, students in close proximity to remind us of our teaching ministry and a natural place for us to drop in.

Lourdes began small with 8 sisters, who could be augmented by those in convalescence and occasionally by relatives. The original building was small, having a dining room, a very restricted community room, a chapel and a couple of offices. It quickly established itself as a good alternative to home-based care and certainly made night nursing a great deal easier. Lourdes sisters who wished, could still attend Mass and office with the Westgate community. This remained an option as long as Lourdes continued.

Gradually we adjusted to increasing needs, medical and Government requirements. In time, Lourdes became a registered Nursing Home, with a capacity of 18. A beautiful new chapel was built, the staff received additional training, more equipment was bought and more rooms became en suite! At this point we were singularly lucky as the religious order Daughters of Jesus were living in Westgate and were happy to take places with us as needed. We continued to go from strength to strength as a Home, finally gaining the Gold Standard Award for End of Life Care in April 2020.

Lourdes was very much part of the Westgate Hub; we visited individuals frequently and shared a great deal of province events together. It was a happy, friendly home. Sadly, it was too small to be cost effective, so we made the hard decision to close. Our Provincial Sister Kathleen, her team, the resident staff at Lourdes and the receiving Care Home in Wanstead took great care over the move. Chestnut Manor staff visited and consulted frequently. By choosing the Care Home in Wanstead it enabled us to keep all Lourdes sisters together which has been a great help to them and to us as most of us are London based. Staff from Lourdes continue to be regular visitors to Wanstead; their arrival brings everyone much joy.

Going to Westgate and walking onto the lawn, to see the chapel and Our Lady of Boulogne *(left)* was like going home. For many of us, Westgate had a profound effect on our lives and we thank God for its 117-year contribution to the Ursuline story.

Westgate Thanksgiving Mass

"How different it must have been for those first sisters who came in 1904 from Boulogne-sur-Mer. Immediately, they began to educate, a process which continues today. A process which will stretch into the future through the legacy given by those holy women, by you my dear sisters and those who have gone before you. On behalf of our Archdiocese I want to express my sincere gratitude for your presence, for your service, for your witness."

Archbishop John Wilson

Sister Theresa Canty

The Ursuline Convent at Westgate served the local communities and the Province, from its foundation in 1904 until its closure in 2021. On 9th July 2021 a Mass of thanksgiving took place in the beautiful and iconic chapel of the Westgate Convent, to celebrate the 117 years of Ursuline presence in Westgate. The chief celebrant was the Archbishop of Southwark John Wilson, he and his secretary, the Reverend Phil Andrews, brought an extra dimension to the day. Concelebrating were ten other priests who had all been associated with the Ursulines at Westgate  over many years. Our Ursuline sisters from across the Province, who all have fond memories and a strong association with Westgate, attended, along with many of our friends.

The Mass was filled with gratitude and joy. The music and readings were all chosen to emphasise our thanksgiving and our hope for whatever the future would bring.

During his sermon, the Archbishop spoke fondly and with great gratitude to the Ursuline community, for their years of dedication to education and prayer. He drew on the lives of St. Ursula and St. Angela Merici, our Foundress. He said that:

"Steeped in the witness of these two saints, it is fidelity to Christ and service to the Church's mission through education, which we celebrate today, in you, and your predecessors, who have sustained the Ursuline presence, here in Westgate for the past 117 years. What an incredible achievement, only possible because of the Lord's call, the Lord's choice, that we, that you, bear fruit that will last."

His final thoughts were to St Angela:

"When it came to speaking about the Christian life, she was refreshingly straight forward: 'Strive to be faithful to that which God has called you', she said. 'Do now what you wish to have done when your moment comes to die.'

'Do something, get moving, risk new things, stick with it, get on your knees, then be ready for big surprises.' This is timeless good advice for every disciple."

After Mass, the Clergy and Ursulines gathered in the community room for refreshments and there was time to catch up with friends, share memories and look to the future.

Although our convent has closed, our Ursuline school continues to educate young people from the area.

'Catholic education is a work of love. Be bound to one another by the bond of charity.'

Lourdes to Wanstead

Sister Colette Traveller

There is no necessity in this account to explain the pain felt by our sisters at leaving the Lourdes Care Home or indeed to tell of the rush of activity needed by Cath Ryan and so many devoted and hardworking staff in Lourdes to ensure our eleven sisters were ready and packed for a journey to Chestnut Manor in Wanstead.
Departure was to be in two groups and the dates given for arrivals the 13th and 17th September 2021. Preparation for the sisters' journeys to Wanstead were planned with Kent County Council to ensure all health and safety procedures were followed.

The eleven Ursuline sisters were to be the first residents to be received in the now larger, 60 bed, newly built and renovated building of Chestnut Manor. Building plans had met with many setbacks due to the Covid Pandemic. A total lockdown early on stopped building completely and then shortages of building materials and supplies resulted in the finishing date being changed several times. But finished it was and passed by the Quality Care Commission for residents to be admitted.

On the morning of 13th September two 'welcome groups' were making the final touches to receiving the sisters. Chestnut Manor had its own team, headed by the Manager. The Home looked beautiful and ready with flowers of welcome everywhere and staff looking their best with smiles and name badges. There was not a builder or decorator in sight but the splendour of their crafts and hard work were there for everyone to see and admire. The chef was busy too, he was in the kitchen making a 'welcome' cake which was much admired and enjoyed by everyone at supper that evening. The second 'welcome' group that morning was a group of Ursuline sisters who set about the task of putting cards and gifts of welcome in each of the sister's rooms. Much thought had gone into getting printed postcards and notelets of the Westgate Garden, Grotto, Chapel and Stations of the Cross. These gifts and cards together with the flowers in each room made a lovely welcome for each sister.

Liam Doogan, the faithful and very expert driver of the loaned minibus, together with Juliette and Lydia, the two carers accompanying the sisters that afternoon, packed the minibus on the morning of 13th September ready for take-off after lunch. The sisters leaving on that first journey to Chestnut Manor were Sisters Mary Ita O'Riordan, Mary Charles Conway, Catherine Pennyfather, Anne Benyon, Emmanuel Bali and Anastasia Nolan. The estimated time of arrival to Wanstead was 4pm. This pattern was replicated on the morning of 17th September for Sisters Veronica Gissing, Gwyn Richards, Mary Carmel Pearce, Mary Murphy and Frances Oakley. The two carers in the bus on 17th were Angelique and Lydia.

On the afternoon of 13th Mrs Joyce Smith arrived before 4pm at Chestnut Manor to become the first resident in the Home. A cheer and clap by the two welcome groups greeted Joyce as she came smiling through the door. Not far behind Joyce was the arrival of the first six Ursuline residents to join Chestnut Manor. Cheers and claps greeted them too and despite them being tired by a long journey from Kent they showed how pleased they were to see and be greeted by the familiar faces of their Ursuline sisters. After greetings in the entrance, willing hands helped to get the sisters in the lift to the 2nd floor and taken to see their rooms for the first time. After an early supper in the dining room and 'new' carers introduced, help was given to open some of those packed items to find the essentials that go to make up a comfortable night. A new room, new carers and a new bed was definitely enough for one day!!

The arrival of the second group of Ursulines on 17th September followed the same pattern as the 13th but of course the sisters in the first group were able to take part in the welcome. Within days, and with the much-appreciated help of the Parish priest, Father Patrick Shannon, Communion Services were arranged. Sister Helen, a sister of Mercy from 'down the road', soon assisted Father Pat with a regular Communion Service every Sunday. Within a very short time, a streamed Mass and Communion was arranged for celebration every Tuesday and Thursday morning with an Ursuline sister present.

Sister Anne Benyon

Sister Anne had the rare incurable disease Myotis Fibrosis, which required constant treatment at Guys over 10 years. Eventually she needed full time care at Lourdes Westgate and then Chestnut Manor at Wanstead. Despite her illness, she remained clear-headed and was very interested in this publication. She followed information from our meetings and all the planning, and was happily about to write on her move from Lourdes to Wanstead. However, she became critically ill on one of her check-up days at Guy's Hospital and died unexpectedly 16th August 2022.

Joyce Smith, who is a resident on a floor where there were 11 Ursuline Sisters became friends with her and asked to write about Anne.

"My first acquaintance with Sr Anne was when the home opened on 13th September 2021. She was very quiet and would sit on her own a lot of the time. One day I asked her why she always sat by herself and said that she should sit with me so that I have someone to talk to. She came over and sat next to me and from then onwards we got on so well.

When we started a knitting club, I asked Anne if she could knit and asked her to join us on a Thursday for our knitting class. She was reluctant to join in but eventually I managed to convince her to come. It turned out that she was a good knitter.

Her brother, Fr Christopher would come and visit Anne and, on those days, we would have a sing along together. Fernanda, who is in charge of activities, brought a keyboard in and I asked Anne if she could play the piano with me. We were all singing together and it was a great afternoon- she loved it.

One afternoon, Fernanda organised a poetry class for us. Although Sr Anne was reluctant at first to take part, she wrote a beautiful poem. The way she recited it to us was amazing and I knew she was an extremely clever lady. She was also extremely talented in her art.

We spoke often about her family, her religious life and her youth. At her funeral it was so lovely to hear her brother speak about how lively she was and how she was sometimes quite naughty!

She regularly spoke about Westgate, about the times walking along the beach. She loved Westgate, I know she was very happy here.

She was always dressed well and wore beautiful blouses- she told me that if I needed one I would have to go to Thailand! We made each other laugh so much, especially at meal times. I never realised how ill Sr Anne was. I knew she went to the hospital for treatment, but she never spoke about being ill or complained- she was a very brave lady. I was very fond of Sr Anne and miss her greatly."

Wanstead One Year On

It would be true to say that moving from Lourdes to Chestnut Manor was one of the hardest things our Sisters have been asked to do. Not only were they to move to a very unfamiliar place, they no longer had the support of a chapel, daily Mass and people who knew them really well. It was a great wrench for the whole province.

God is good and has supported us so well over the last eighteen months. The presence of the Ursulines in Chestnut Manor is greatly valued. The Sisters have made good friends with the staff and residents. They are fortunate to have an on-line Mass three times a week for all catholic residents. Ursulines and Sr. Helen (a Sister of Mercy) takes communion to the Sisters; which is greatly appreciated. The local parish priest has also visited, so the Sisters have been able to receive and be supported by the sacraments of the sick and reconciliation.

Our Special Homemaker, Maria Martins, supports the Sisters on a daily basis. She takes them shopping, for a walk in the area (taking in the Coffee Shop), to medical appointments and generally is a trusted friend. The Home provides a variety of activities and themed events.

The Sisters are now settled in Wanstead and enjoy numerous visits from Ursulines and their many friends. Chestnut Manor can never replace Lourdes, but it comes a close second.

"My last word to you, is that you live in harmony, united together, all of one heart and one will"
-St Angela Merici

The Reality of change

In our brainstorming for "Embracing our Future" we appreciated we had been well informed, consulted, and in agreement that re-organisation and closures were necessary. Communities where the axe finally fell were grateful that they were told in person by the Provincial and Team., but reality of closure remained, and a group found itself spontaneously sharing. This was captured on tape.

Sister Vianney Connolly

We had 10 difficult months to get used to the idea that Shotton was closing but we knew from the Province day in 2014- that it was obvious we had to do something drastic. We had all been prepared, it didn't come out of the blue - but we didn't want to be the first. In the end change came to all of us.

After 10 years of being just two sisters, moving wasn't easy, we had had a great deal of freedom and we had to be open with each other to make it work. We built on what was already established. and were very involved in the local community, with Justice and Peace and Fair Trade. We made many friends and our house was always open. We welcomed people weekly.

We came down to Forest Gate on 20th October- driven down by a Serviam member and her husband. A parishioner packed more than we could have managed. It was hard to get rid of furniture etc. I came to an unknown parish and environment but I felt the wind of St Ursula helping me make the move and trust in God.

We had a great send off from the local Fair-Trade group who were very active in Shotton and the parish. People came to wave us off and make sure we were ok. Our house was their house. Letting go was like a bereavement- I found great insecurity, I missed the openness of living with just one other person. When I came to Forest Gate it was very different, it was hard to adjust to a different community and their way of doing things. I grew to appreciate the parish and community but it took a long time to adjust.

Sister Jayne Horswill

My experience of leaving was a big wrench- I was very happy and we had a thriving apostolate. But for me, throughout my life I had moved so many times and I saw it as just another move. It was painful but it was a move towards a new beginning. An ending is always difficult but it wasn't traumatic. The Greenwich community was there to receive us and were open to receiving us which made the move easier. We had a leaving Mass and there was a piece of music that was written specially for us.

Sister Kathy Glencross

It is hard for other communities to accept new members- Greenwich was three and then doubled with three of us from Lancaster. But I never felt unwanted or that it was a problem but it is important to acknowledge the pain of leaving a community, it's a grief that you don't expect. Each community is different- and it is hard for them as it also upsets their way of doing things.

Sister Felicity Young

At Ilford we lived a very different life to the more structured life of Forest Gate. We were free and independent, it was an easy lifestyle. We used the house lots for retreats and spiritual direction. It was a beautiful house, sunny and bright and it had a lovely garden. I visited the shops to do street pastoring, I felt safe in the local area and was very fond of the local parish. It was hard to leave after 18 years and to move into a different environment.

Sister Colette Traveller

Westgate closure started with the community. More and more sisters were moving into the Lourdes Care Home and it was eroding the community. The numbers in the main community were going down as our state of health and age was in decline. The top floor of the community became empty, we turned off the phones, stopped providing our own dinner and shared that of the Lourdes community. Eventually we started to think about closing. Our biggest trauma was leaving the chapel and setting up the community room for Mass. It was a very painful time. In November 2019 the community closed and in December Beatrice went to Greenwich and I moved to Forest Gate. Theresa stayed in Brescia with Alice so that there was continuity in looking after Lourdes. By February 2020 Covid was upon us with its lockdown. So, all in all this was a turbulent period.

Sister Una McCreesh

My position is unusual. I have only moved once, and have in fact spent 40 years in what for me has been an ever-evolving Forest Gate, a place that I know and love. I realise how painful, difficult and costly the reality of diminishment has been for the very many who have been uprooted.

It is 30 years since the Forest Gate community moved "across the Garden" from St George's Road to Grosvenor Road. A year later we felt we needed to come together to take stock of what difference it had made.to us. I still remember how therapeutic we all found that occasion and how everybody contributed.

At that time, there were 16 of us. I think our composition has changed every year since; our numbers have been as low as 3 and currently are 8. So constant change has been our reality, as to who we are, what we do, and the building adjustments we have needed.

We have gained in our appreciation and understanding of each other both as a province, a community and individually, by the professional guidance we have received from Father John Foley, and by the follow on sharing we have done together.

"If, according to times and circumstances, the need arises to make new rules or do something differently, do it prudently and with good advice"

-St Angela Merici

Our Province Community

Alongside the pain and heartache of closing houses we have also received many blessings. As a province we have developed a generosity of spirit and a readiness to face the future together. In times past we may have been rather reluctant to speak at a province meeting when there were fifty or sixty of us. Since 2014, not only have our numbers decreased but, because we have had so many meetings and social gatherings, we are now more relaxed and enjoy one another's company.

Sisters Angela Cronin and Jackie Doherty at a Province meeting 2022

Our Ursuline Legacy

From their first arrival in this country, our Ursuline sisters aimed to immerse themselves in the environment where they found themselves but they were also prepared to take stock of local circumstances and to adjust accordingly.

In this random archival record, we see how that adaptation was played out, in the sisters' ordinary lives. From their beginning, they strove to provide an education that was comparable to local provision. In the post 1944 period, when Secondary Education became available for all, they agreed to accept the constraints and benefits of Government support, to make Catholic secondary education widely available.

The post Vatican II group also learned to live through a period of dramatic change. In the **Shaken to our roots** section, to which each sister alive when we began this work has contributed, shows clearly how ultimately change was welcomed.

Today in a very different postmillennial world, we are called upon to face the ending of our present lifestyle, using the same courage our first sisters had in beginning it.

We have been engaged in working together in shaping that ending, firstly providing for our own physical diminishment and by creating our legacy for the future. building on the courage and foresight of our Ursuline family for the past one hundred years.

We have strengthened the bonds which unite the schools by the introduction of the Ursuline virtues. Our Ursuline Links charity continues to attract young people to give service beyond their school years.

In this section we will look at:

Ursuline Schools Today

Ursuline Education Community

Ursuline Links

The picture below seems an appropriate introduction to this section

Ursuline Schools Today

Education in its many forms has been at the heart of our Ursuline lives. The first Ursulines who came to England from a variety of lands made schools their priority. A number of those early schools are still educating students who bring their gifts and talents to enrich the lives of their peers.

Vital to any school is its ethos. In times past, Ursulines ran and staffed the schools themselves. Over the years, the Sisters withdrew, but the Ursuline charism remains. We pay tribute to the current Headteachers and staff in today's schools. They keep the gospel message and St Angela's spirit at the heart of all they do. Students and staff from diverse backgrounds and faiths enrich the school communities and aim to go out in service to others. "Serviam", once adopted, never leaves them.

 St Angela's Forest Gate

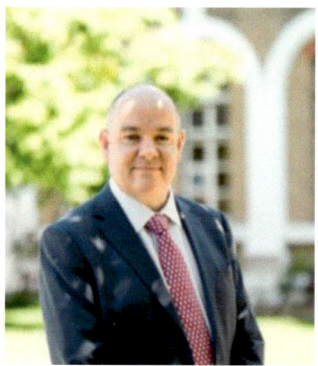

Head Teacher
Mark Johnson

SCHOOL HISTORY	
1862	Upton Boarding School
1862	Elementary day school
1879	St Angela's began as a Grammar School
1904	St Antony's Primary School
1923	School recognised by Board of Education
1945	Became: Multilateral Voluntary Aided
1975	Multi-lateral became Comprehensive
1983	St Angela's and St Bonaventure's VIth Form
1992	Diocese of Brentwood joint Trustees
1992	Diocese became sole trustees
2015	St Angela's V1th Form opened
2017	Desenzano V1th form wing opened

Through our curriculum and community life, we seek to meet the needs of the whole person and to enable all to achieve their full potential.

We offer to all the challenge of building and living in a community in which members are equally valued

We share with St Angela's a commitment to the service of young people, which will empower them to play their full part in society.

Parents we invite you to play a part in our vibrant community where 'Serviam' is at the heart of all we do .

Time Capsule Buried
8th May 21012
To mark the 150th anniversary of the school

St Ursula's Greenwich

Head Teacher
Ursula Norbert

SCHOOL HISTORY

1877	Ursuline Sisters arrive from Duderstadt
1822	Some Sisters went to Australia and founded Armidale
1892	Ursulines from Gravelines took over the school
1920	Admitted scholarship pupils
1935	Became a two-form entry Grammar School
1949	Became a voluntary aided Grammar
1997	Became a three form entry Comprehensive School 11-18

By the time they leave an Ursuline school our students will be aware of Christ as the centre of their lives.

Be willing in the spirit of SERVIAM to develop their talents and use them for the good of others especially the most needy.

Be friendly, happy and confident and able to work with patience and generosity assured that with God they can do great things.

Be focused on Justice and Peace as they keep alive gospel values in today's world.

Be able to recognise the uniqueness of each one by showing respect and love for all.

Be happy to know St. Angela and to have shared her values in the context of our Ursuline School.

Statue of St Ursula in the foyer

Ursuline Academy Ilford

Head Teacher
Fiona Stone

SCHOOL HISTORY

- 1903 Ursuline High School was founded from Forest Gate
- 1943 Ursuline Convent established in lford
- 1944 Ilford became independent from Forest Gate
- 1945 The school became Direct Grant enabling 50% of places to be free.
- 1999 Became Voluntary Aided Secondary School
- 2006 Became State Funded Academy in the Diocese of Brentwood.

We are a Catholic community of faith, love and service rooted in the spirit of St Angela.
Through Christ and the Gospel and in our diverse community we strive to provide an environment for young women to flourish, spiritually, academically and socially.
We are a vibrant faith community inspired by our founder Angela Merici, whose motto "Serviam- I will serve"lies at the heart of our daily routine and practice .

Commemorative Icon created by students for commissioning of
Fiona Stone
22nd March 2033

Ursuline College Westgate

SCHOOL HISTORY

1904	Sisters came from Boulogne sur Mer
1906	They purchased Hatton House
1926	These Sisters returned to France
1926	Ursulines from Bideford bought the school
1948	Sister Anne Benyon 1st Kent Scholarship
1995	School became Co-ed
1998	School became a Diocesan Comprehensive
2004	Sports College
2015	Joined Kent Catholic Schools Partnership

Head Teacher
Danielle Lancefield

We are pleased to be part of a national and worldwide network of Ursuline schools, where we share common goals, academic excellence, a spirit of service, care and development of young people.

SERVIAM, underpins every aspect of our school.

Like JESUS we aim to listen, respond, heal encourage, forgive, comfort, teach and challenge

Angela patron of Ursuline schools worldwide calls on us to make our school a place where relationships goodness and kindness.

Statue of St Angela
in the chapel
by
Phillip Lindsay Clarke

Ursuline High Wimbledon

Head Teacher
Julia Waters

SCHOOL HISTORY

1892 School founded from Forest Gate
1936 School recognised as efficient by The Board of Education
1936 Scholarship pupils admitted
1948 School became a voluntary aided grammar
1969 School became a 13-18 Comprehensive
1988 Joint V!th form with Wimbledon Jesuit College
2006 Dorothy Kazel Building was opened

Inspired by the life and work of Saint Angela Merici, our Ursuline school commits itself to education for tomorrow's world within the dynamic tradition of Catholic belief and practice.

As a Christian community, characterised by a spirit of respect, trust and joy, we promote excellence in every aspect of life, thereby fully developing each individual.

We are delighted to be part of a worldwide network of Ursuline schools and work with our students to deepen our links with other Ursuline students, both here in the UK, and across the world.

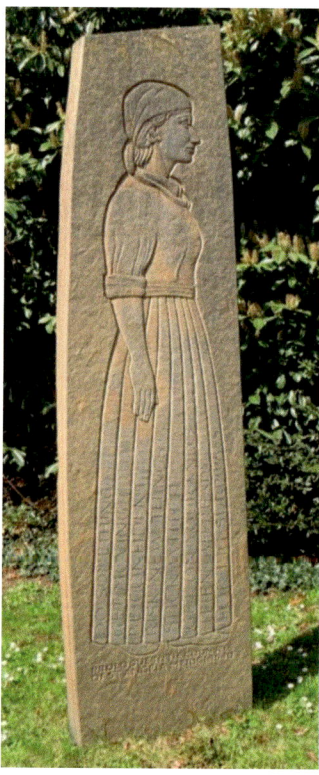

Commissioned statue of St Angela with text in the folds of her dress

 Headteacher
Lorraine Pereira

The Ursuline school has always encouraged my fellow students and I to strive for excellence and to always try our best. Whether it be RE or literacy, Ursuline children put their all into everything. Our values have taught us to persevere and to listen to our conscience, even when we desire not to. Our values are not only good pieces of advice to follow, but they are rules for life as well. For example, we have learnt to be discerning and to know the difference between good and bad. Skills like these can guide us through our journeys in life and teach us how to grow into mature adults. Likewise, our values explain to us how we should behave in school and towards one another. Kindness is key, and our positivity can shine throughout our entire school community. We are taught that even a smile can go a long way. As a school, we intend on keeping everybody happy and keen to learn for the whole school day. At Ursuline, we consider ourselves a community and in our community you can find togetherness, friendship and love towards one another. Our motto is: "Once an Ursuline, always an Ursuline."

Our Ursuline Values by Amelia Hussain (Yr 6)

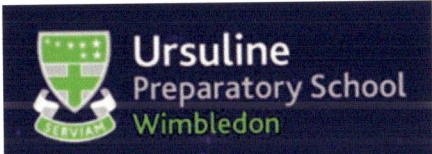 Headteacher
Caroline Molina

We place equal value on the education of the heart, the mind and the soul, in the sure and certain knowledge that only through the equal development of all three can you truly become the person you were born to be; the best that you can be. Two words dominate this school, Serviam and Insieme. Both words were central to the teachings of St Angela. Every girl and boy at our school knows about Serviam, the importance to be of service to others and Insieme, the joy and strength of working together for the individual and the community.

Ursuline Education Community

Ursuline Education Community was launched in all eight schools in England in September 2019, with the intention of codifying the very essence of an Ursuline education and expressing it through the Ursuline Student Profile. The profile is informed by and is based on the writings of St Angela Merici and reflects her devotion to and promotion of Catholic formation and virtues.

The aim of the Ursuline Pupil Profile (USP) is "to produce a profile that describes the whole process of Ursuline education, rather than that of a school leaver." The central symbol is a tree, which is a powerful and recurring symbol in the writings of St Angela.

The fruit on the USP tree takes the form of ten leaves. Two of the leaves bear the guiding principles of Angela Merici, namely "United in Harmony" and "Serviam", each of the other eight leaves bear a pair of virtues, all linked to St Angela's writings and to her life.

Together, the ten leaves of the Ursuline Student Profile propose what a student in an Ursuline school grows to be and very importantly, what the school needs to do to nurture and develop that growth. Therefore, the image is accompanied by two sets of formal statements: one set for the students, the other set of statements for the school.

The image and **student statements** are designed to provide a rich resource to stimulate student engagement through discussion, exploration, reflection, prayer in assemblies and liturgies, in charity work, in practical endeavour in and out of school.

The image and the **school statements** are designed to guide the work of governors, school leaders, teachers, support staff and of course parents, as the USP should be used to explain to current and prospective parents the essence of Ursuline education. It takes two years to work through the

Ursuline Student Profile, starting in the autumn term of one school year, with a term long focus on "United in Harmony" and finishing with a term long focus on "Serviam" at the end of the following school year.

Each school has a UEC representative, and they meet once a term to plan and to share resources. Students are also involved, with Year 10 representatives meeting to share ideas and experiences twice a year.

School to school visits called "United in Mission" provide an opportunity to share the different ways in which both the Ursuline Education Community and the Ursuline Student Profile are being used and developed in a mutually supportive and enriching manner.

The Ursulines are very grateful to the Jesuits, and particularly to Fr Adrian Porter SJ, for their generosity in sharing their work on the Jesuit Institute and the Pupil Profile. However, UEC would never have come to birth had not Fidelma Boyd been willing to accept the challenge to " get moving and risk new things" to create this legacy.

Experience of UEC
A United in Mission visit

Ms Ursula Norbert- Headteacher of St Ursula's, Greenwich

It was a pleasure to spend the day at St Angela's, as part of a visiting team. On the day, I had the opportunity to speak with staff, drop into lessons, watch a Year 7 assembly and meet with 6th formers.

Students at St Angela's have a voice. It was amazing to meet with the 'Super 6' students, who were part of a small nurture group. The 'Super 6' are in Year 7. They have a safe space, feel happy and know that this small environment is just for them. Students were confident to discuss their journey and how helpful the school is to ensure that their time at the school is enjoyable and education is accessible. Although students are part of a small group, they feel included. Staff are experienced in teaching students in such an unusual setting. Students were happy to talk about how they had all grown in confidence by working in a small group and preparing to graduate into the mainstream. This is one good example of how a school can close the gap.

While walking the school site, it was great to see so many quotes that are linked to "Serviam" and the Ursuline virtues. It was also interesting to note that Departments all have a leaf linked to virtues, giving them their own identity. The displays made the environment warm as well as very welcoming. Walking around enabled me to take away many ideas that could be used in my own school environment. I could see many traits of an Ursuline school.

The Rise Up Day gave Year 10 students an opportunity to put arguments forward about peer pressure in such an articulate way.

6th form students said that they quickly adjusted to their new environment and felt very welcome. They had bought into the Ursuline values and were very proud to be part of the school community, no matter their faith.

Ofsted Feedback

The school was inspected in November 2022 and had been planning for the visit for many years. The Deputy Head shared her Ofsted experience and was able to discuss how the 'deep dives' were carried out and how prepared staff had to be. She also discussed the sporting life of the school and the importance of tracking groups of students. For example, the type of sports activities that SEND students participate in after school and which students have Chrome books. She also stressed the importance of tracking everything that they do. For example, all the enrichment activities that take place. This session was very valuable for me as we are due an Ofsted visit any time now. It was evident that the hard work had paid off as the school achieved an Outstanding judgement.

It was a pleasure to visit the school.

"Seek to spread peace and concord wherever you are."

-St Angela Merici

A day at Wintershall

As part of the celebrations leading up to the 100 year anniversary of the English Ursulines joining the Roman Union five Ursuline schools took part in a day's retreat which was organised at Wintershall, a working farm and Catholic retreat centre in the countryside near Guildford, Surrey. The day was for year 6 and 7 students.

The Wintershall education team led a day of drama, art and reflection. At the start of the day Lucy Hall (the Education officer at Wintershall and an Ursuline alumna!) spoke with the students about the Ursuline virtues and what it means to live them on a daily basis.

There was a drama in which Mary Magdalene wondered about what would have happened if people hadn't believed her resurrection experience and this was linked then to the life of St Angela, and how one woman's story and vision can change the lives of thousands (or millions) of people.

The students then broke into smaller groups and were taken for a walk around the estate in which they met different animals and could reflect on the connection between the animals the life of Christ and the Ursuline virtues.

They wrote their reflections on leaves which were later added to a tree which Sr Kathleen will bring to the Jubilee Mass in October. They were shown a 1000 year-old tree and could touch it and were asked to think about the connection we have with all people in time and across the world now. The students also had an opportunity to create a work of art (based on the Serviam badge) which we then used in the reflection time at the end of the day.

Two students reflect on the day:
"On this trip, we met other Ursuline schools, which helped us understand that we are all a massive community because although we all have a different school uniform, different teachers, different schools and have never met each other before, we all had one thing in common. Our UEC Virtues and most importantly our school motto "Serviam". It was truly an educational day full of courage and inspiration."

"We went on a nature walk to the stations of the cross. Each was ornate and beautiful but my favourite was the tomb of Christ represented by intertwining tree roots. It really showed the beauty and love in the sacrifice of Jesus. From this final activity we received a cross which I think is a wonderful way to remember the entire experience of the day. This whole experience was a deeper dive in to what it means to be a Christian as someone who isn't of that faith. As a Hindu, I think that in my faith we also believe that a simple life is one of the best ways to live and that love and compassion are some of the main qualities that should be in a person.

Ursuline Links

Our Youth Project, Ursuline Links, came to birth in summer 2010 when a group of teachers, students and Ursulines went to New Orleans, USA to help rebuild homes after Hurricane Katrina.

Since then, apart from the covid years, students and adults have continued to give service in many parts of the world: India, South Africa, USA (three different locations), Ireland and England.

Young people aged 17+ mostly come from Ursuline schools in Ilford, Brentwood, Forest Gate, Wimbledon and Westgate. Under the guidance of the Ursuline Links staff they attend a monthly meeting from September to June. These meetings, including a Discipleship Day and a Retreat Day, are carefully planned to engage the students in self-reflection, prayer and action.

These months of preparation lead to a service project to be undertaken during the summer holidays. Projects have been located in Care Homes, Day Camps, Food Banks, Homeless Centres to name but a few. We went to New Orleans for more than ten years to help rebuild homes. In India the students taught English to young children.

These projects give young people the chance to work together for the benefit of others. During this time, they are able to work, pray, relax and have a good time together. It helps them to develop their understanding of how we embody gospel values in our lives today. We welcome students and supporting adults from a variety of faiths. Prayer and reflection play a central part in all we do. We ensure that all spiritual activities are inclusive and relevant to all participants.

Polish Sisters Experience of Ursuline Links

Summer in Forest Gate by Sister Monika Pławecka

This summer, thanks to the European exchange programme, Sr. Katarzyna Starek and I spent one month in the Forest Gate community, taking part in some of the Ursuline Links projects. It was truly an enriching and beautiful experience so I'd like to share just some of the most precious memories I have from this time.

The very first thing which struck my attention was great national, cultural and religious diversity visible and tangible all around the Forest Gate area. At the same time I experienced this environment- our neighbours, parishioners, foreigners- as a very open and welcoming space. That, together with great hospitality and kindness of sisters of the Forest Gate community, made me feel at home very quickly.

Then came the time of our work and involvement with the Ursuline Links. The biggest event of that time was certainly Day Camp run at Forest Gate for 30 children aged 7-11. I took part in preparations before the Day Camp, in the Camp itself and then in big cleaning and sorting-out action after the end of it. We had 18 students who – after a year of training and formation- made their commitment to give up a week of their holidays and to serve the children during the Camp. Though coming from different schools, after a short while they made a wonderful team, serving and having fun together. Each evening we concluded our day of service with some prayer, reflection and sharing. We ended our week deeply grateful for all we had experienced, learnt and shared together.

The second project that we were involved in was the one on Social Justice. In small groups of 4-6 students and an accompanying adult we were visiting different kinds of places and organisations dealing with social justice issues and working with them as volunteers. Girls who took part in the project could get the experience of some service in the Care Home, food banks, welcome centres, etc. Challenged in many different ways, we tried to put the spirit of Ursuline SERVIAM into practice.

Time flies and so did our month at Forest Gate. We were blessed with many different opportunities and invitations to encounter God in the midst of daily realities of that community, in apostolic work, during the time of rest and sightseeing, in surprises and unexpected meetings, enjoying beauty and diversity around.

Great thanks to God and our dear sisters: Kathleen, Una, Margaret, Felicity, Vianney, Theresa, Colette, Catherine and Zela!

Last Word

St Angela Merici our foundress
A woman who wanted
consecrated life but did not
want convent or monastery.

A woman who told her
followers
"Act, bestir yourselves"
yet took forty years
to take action herself.

A woman who did not found
a religious congregation
yet is regarded
as foundress of the Ursulines

A woman who never taught,
yet is regarded as a great
educator.

A woman who loved
and was loved much.
And has promised to be with us
"To the end of Time"

List of Our Sisters

1923-2023

Adrian MacKinnon
Adrienne Cranch
Agatha O'Brien
Agnes Casey
Adrian MacKinnon
Agnes Joseph Padmore
Agnes Ross
Ailbe Quane
Alice Montgomery
Alison Marjoribanks (Hugh)
Aloysia McCarthy
Aloysius Browne
Aloysius Worthington
Alphonse Taczanowska
Alphonsus Coleman
Alphonsus Fitzpatrick
Alphonsus Mulligan
Ambrose Reidy
Anastasia Nolan (Joachim)
Andrea Bayliss
Andrew Byron
Angela Bowen
Angela Callaghan
Angela Cody
Angela Cronin
Angela Dunlea
Angela Fuchs
Angela Mary Reidy

Ann Godfrey (Baptist)
Anne Benyon (Thecla)
Anne Casey
Anne Curley
Anne Marie Le Bayon
Anne Marie Petit
Anne O'Riordan
Anne-Marie Gardiner
Anthony Lawrence
Antoinette Carroll
Antonia Ashpole
Antony Dunbar
Antony Murray
Antony O'Neill
Antony Rushe
Aquinas Hunt
Aquinas Langridge
Armida Veglio
Augustine Collins
Augustine Gerard
Augustine Murphy
Austin Gay
Baptiste O'Hanlon
Barbara Redmond
Beatrice Garnett
Benedict Davies
Benedict Dempsey
Benedict Ward

Berchmans Clarke
Berchmans Evans
Bernadette Frost
Bernadette Rennison
Bernard Burchart
Bernard Flood
Bonaventure Jackson
Bonaventure Kelly
Bonaventure Scanlan
Brendan Finnegan
Brendan O'Riordan
Brigid Sheehy
Campion O'Hagan
Catherine Kelly (Alban)
Catherine Pennyfather
Cecilia Cremonini
Cecilia Mary Churchman
Cecilia Thomas
Cecily Banwell
Celine Murray
Charles Billing
Christina Cleary
Christopher Whitehead
Clare Brown
Clare Horspool
Clare Tanter
Clement Cunningham
Clotilde Griffin

Colette Traveller
Columba Cleary
Columba Finnegan
Columba Mulcahy
Columba O'Keefe
Columba Reidy
Coralie Walsh (Martin)
Cuthbert McGrail
Damien O'Mahony
De Sales Murray
Delphine Reithmuller
Dolores Caine
Dominic Blake
Dominic Gleeson
Dominic Tizard
Dorothea Dawson (Bede)
Dorothea Rigby
Dorothy Perrott (Brendan)
Edmund Crawley
Elizabeth Campbell (Joseph Mary)
Elizabeth Clarke
Elizabeth Reithmuller
Elizabeth Vincent
Elizabeth Watkins
Elizabeth Wedekind
Emmanuel Bali
Ethelbyrga Beedom
Etheldreda Gray

Eucharia Padbury
Euchariste Vantorre
Eugene Ryan
Eugenie Carey
Eustochiam Eward
Felicity Young (Austin)
Finbarr Murnane
Frances Browne (Simon)
Frances Oakley
Francis Hart
Francis Lemarchand
Francis O'Toole
Francis Stoner
Francisca Needler
Gabriel Mary Parry
Gabriel Ryan
Gabrielle O'Brien
George Scott
Gerard Donovan
Gerard Fyten
Gerard Gill
Gerard Marie Guthbier
Gerard Marie Guthier
Gertrude Browne
Gertrude Burns
Gertrude Kearney
Gertrude Lemaire
Gertrude Mary Roche

Gertrude Richards
Gregory Hannon
Gwyn Richards
Helen Newton
Helene Declerck
Henry Pendlebury
Ignatius Hammond
Ignatius Higginson
Ignatius Lawrence
Ignatius Stone
Imelda Carey
Imelda Grew
Imelda McCartney
Jacqueline Doherty
Jacques Jennebach
Jayne Horswill (Aelred)
Jenefer Glencross (Raphael)
Joachin Bancquarest
Joan Keitch (Luke)
John Baptist Shaw
John Berchmans Clarke
John Berchmans Gutbier
John Berchmans L'Empereur
John Fawl
John Stahl
Joseph Hammersley
Joseph Major
Joseph O'Reilly

Joseph Powell
Joseph Rowntree
Joseph Ryan
Joseph Scott-Murray
Josephine Baird
Josephine Gray
Josephine White
Julienne Bolger
Katharine Glencross
Kathleen Colmer (Vladimir)
Kathleen England
Kieran Harvey
Kieran Hawe
Kieran O'Riordan
Kwyrina Karas
Lamberta Griffiths
Laurentine Watkins
Lawrence McCann
Louis Marie Ryan
Louis Stephenson
Loyola Keogh
Loyola Wilson
Lucy Alcock
Lucy Bonington (Bernard)
Lucy Muller
M.M du S. Sacrement Deltour
Magdalen Bellasis
Magdalen Cleary

Magdalen Jackson
Magdalen Nicole
Magdalena Tully
Margaret Churchman (Stanislaus)
Margaret Higgs
Margaret Lemmon (Aidan)
Margaret Lyth (John)
Margaret Marie Debusschere
Margaret Mary Horsman
Margaret Mary Lumley
Margaret Mary McCann
Margaret Rolfe (John Bosco)
Marguerite Marie Bonnet
Maria Goretti Fitzpatrick
Marie de Jesus Sanders
Marie De L'Incarntion Varlet
Marie des Agnes Brunaque
Marie Des Anges Dahmann
Marie Gertrude Burns
Marie Raphael Wood
Marie Therese McGeough
Marie Therese Pommier
Marta Napierata
Martha Gregson
Martha Van Der Laus
Martha Vandenaus
Marthe Jouin
Mary Agnes Brumagne

Mary Agnes Podmore
Mary Alphonsus Lee
Mary Angela Boord
Mary Augustine Sharman
Mary Bridget Brazill
Mary Campion Gibson
Mary Carmel Pearce
Mary Catherine Connolly
Mary Catherine Flannagan
Mary Cecilia Murray
Mary Charles Conway
Mary Elizabeth Port
Mary Francis Brocklehurst
Mary Francis Burns
Mary Gonzaga Anderson
Mary Ita O'Riordan
Mary Joseph Weddall
Mary Magdalen Hogan
Mary Martha McCann
Mary Monica Tannam
Mary Murphy
Mary of the Incarnation Welch
Mary of the Rosary Clayton
Mary -Sacred Heart Buffechoux
Mary Paul Quane
Mary Roch Glockner
Mary Spellman
Mary Veronica Rennison

Mary Winefride Sturman
Mary Zita Walsh
Mathilde Smits
Matthew Horsman
Maureen Cloonan (Bernardine)
Maureen Coyne (Canisius)
Maureen Moloney (Miriam)
Mechtilde de Helden
Michael Finch
Michael Murphy
Mildred Reidy
Monica Henniker
Monica Kearney
Monica Kimberley
Monica Roberts
Moya Lemmon (John Berchmans)
Patricia Coyne
Patricia Cummings (Vincent)
Patricia Hoyne
Patricia Quigley
Patrick Begley
Patrick O'Sullivan
Paul Flood
Paul Fuller
Paul Vidler
Peter Buck
Peter Rimmer
Philippe Cahill
Philomena Carroll
Philomena Grady

Pia Gombos
Pierre King
Providence Pochet
Regis Woodlock
Richard Thompson
Rita Faria
Roch Hasleden
Rodriguez Wiersma
Rosaire Jouin
Rose Rattigan
Rose Tomlinson
Rosemary Chambers (Gerard)
Salesia Campbell
Scholastica Muller
Scholastica Whelan
St Candide Delwaulle
St Ignatius Lawrens
St Joseph Lammin
St Mary Alexander
St Pierre Vergriete
St Redempteur Champagne
Stanislaus Perron
Stephen Woodley
Teresa Flynn
Teresa Neylan
Teresita Clemo
Terisita Lightfood
Theodore Rudge
Theresa Canty (Robert)
Therese Anderson

Thomas More Elsmore
Una McCreesh (Sebastian)
Ursula Cooper
Ursula Daly
Ursula Duffield
Ursula Szudey
Veronica Gissing
Veronica Hammond
Veronica Lyden (Mechtilde)
Veronica MacDonald
Veronica Mary Phillips (Jude)
Veronica Paddison
Vianney Archard
Vianney Connolly (Philomena)
Victor Cooren
Vincent Cunningham
Vincent Feeley
Vincent McCarthy
Vincent Vantorre
Winifred Antill
Winifred Flyter
Winifrid Booth
Xavier Bond
Xavier Callaghan
Xavier Mullin
Xavier Rowntree
Zela Procter (Carmel)
Zita Murray
Zita Wall

Pre 1923

Mere Anne Marie Petit

Mere de l'Annunciation Pierens

Mere Laurentina Blankonsteiner

Mere Margerite Marie de Busschere

Mère St Fr.d'Assise Laprise

Mere Ste Mechtilde de Huden

Mother Agnes Gredwood

Mth Agatha Engelke

Mth Agatha Langdale

Mth Agnes Caroline Paasch

Mth Almin M.Joseph de Marseul

Mth Angela Jaegar

Mth Angela Jefferys

Mth Anna Kellner

Mth Antonia Soehlmann

Mth Augustin Sieber

Mth Augustine Jackson

Mth Augustine Wideman

Mth Badier M. Berchmans Loiseau

Mth Bernard Wippern

Mth Boniface Buker

Mth Boniface Freckman

Mth Caroline Cordula

Mth Catherine Coppin

Mth Cecile Higgs

Mth M. Augustine Halle

Mere Ste Gertrude Lemaire

Mth Cecily Stromeyer

Mth Charles Turley

Mth Clare Straker

Mth Crescentia Cools

Mth de la Presentation Shaw

Mth Dominic Haddy

Mth Eugenia MacNamara

Mth Flavia Delporte

Mth Francis de Sales Vandamme

Mth Francois D'Assise Hugnet

Mth Francois De Sales Prevost

Mth Genovefa Welfes

Mth Germaine MacDiarmid

Mth Germaine Tintillier

Mth Gertrude Connolly

Mth Hildegard von Hagen

Mth Ignatia Crone

Mth Ignatius Maher

Mth John Berchmans Nolan

Mth John Morrall

Mth Justine Barthel

Mth Kieran Harre

Mth Louis Bathilde

Mth Louis Dejonghe

Mth Lucie Leclerq

Mth M Cecilia Smith

Mth M. De la Croix Le Dantec

Mth Xavier Hynes

Rev Mth Maria Theresa Lecaille

Rev Mth Marie Di Jesus Belloc

Rev Mth St Fr.de Sales Thibault

Rev Mth St Ursule Lardeur

Soeur Ste Angele Corbin

Soeur Marie Ange Pelouin

Soeur St Andre Patry

Soeur St Charles Heurtaut

Soeur St Etienne Desavoye

Soeur St Paul Brulay

Soeur Ste Agnes le Bouteiller

Soeur Ste Germaine Almin

Soeur Ste Gertrude Pelouin

Soeur Ste Marthe Galicher

Soeur Ste Veronique Lestang

Sr Alice Coatval

Sr Aloysius Lacey

Sr Anastasia Lamy

Sr Anastasie Delbecque

Sr Anne Fretel

Sr Anne Marie de Jesus Frolich di Maretti

Sr Anne Marie Guillon

Sr Anne Marie Rochard

Sr Anthony Beedom

Sr Antoine Lahaye

Sr Avoie Ciray

Sr Bernadette Rose

Sr Brigette Taelman

Sr Camille Lamy

Sr Cordula Lange

Sr Ephraim Chicot

Sr Felis Geffroy

Sr Genevieve Willaert

Sr Gertrude Besson

Sr Hyacinthe Lamy

Sr Joseph Le Royer

Sr Josephine Grimshaw

Sr Josephine Porquet

Sr Julienne Hoenvenaars

Sr Louis de Gonzague

Sr Margaret Mary Hedley

Sr Marie Amand

Sr Marie Angele Broquaine

Sr Marie Berchmans Loiseau

Sr Marie Bernard Mancel

Sr Marie Celestine Lamy

Sr Marie de l'Incarnation Derieux

Sr Marie de St Laurent Coursin

Sr Marie Guichoux

Sr Marie Joseph de Marseul

Sr Marie Madeleine Vastel

Sr Marie Quinton

Sr Marie Thérèse Raine

Sr Martha Boeven

Sr Mary Agnes Podmore

Mth M. De L'Incarnation Derieux

Mth M. De St Alphonse Hossard

Mth M. De St Ignace Loiseau

Mth M. De St Jean Dorey

Mth M. De St Laurent Coursin

Mth M. Du Calvaire Boyer

Mth M. Du St Sacrement Mauger

Mth M.Du Sacré Coeur Vautier

Mth Madeleine Vastel

Mth Magdalen Beckers

Mth Marie de l'Incarnation Bourgois

Mth Marie St Louis de Gonzaque Boucherry

Mth Marie Vandamme

Mth Martha Rudolph

Mth Mary Augustine Joyce

Mth Mary Joseph de Busschere

Mth Mary Martin

Mth Mary of the Incarnation Galvan

Mth Mary Shaw

Mth Mary Xavier Green

Mth Patry Marie de Jésus Béguin

Mth Philomena Abbott

Mth Philomena Keily

Mth St Angela Marais

Mth St Berchmans Evans

Mth St Bernard Kelly

Mth Visitation Crowe

Mth St Charles Billing

Mth St Etienne Gilles

Mth St Hyacinthe Eiffie

Mth St Ignace Higginson

Mth St Jean de la Croix Mathieu

Mth St Jean l'Evangeliste Morrall

Mth St Jules Fromentin

Mth St Louis de Gonzague Stephenson

Mth St Patrick O'Sullivan

Mth St Stanislas Maudin

Mth St Stanislaus Dubas

Mth Ste Angele Malsallez

Mth Ste Angèle Moulin

Mth Ste Claire Lechauve

Mth Ste Genevieve Saget

Mth Ste Lucie Saget

Mth Ste Madeleine Hogan

Mth Ste Marie Sonnois

Mth Ste Ursule

Mth Theresa Keseling

Mth Therese Masselis

Mth Thomas Aquinas Todd

Mth Ursula Crone

Mth Ursula Crone

Mth Ursula Keily

Mth Victoria Van der Auwera

Mth Vincent Spurgeon

Sr Mary Alexis Touce
Sr Mary Jackson
Sr Monica Tully
Sr Monique Tavernier
Sr Nathalie Fichant
Sr Pierre Noel
Sr Rosalie Geffroy
Sr St Andre Pabry
Sr St Antoine Beal
Sr St Etienne Desavoye
Sr St F.d'Assise Laprise
Sr St Famille Noedts
Sr St Frances Lemarchant
Sr St Francoise Masson
Sr St Jean Baptiste Badier
Sr St Joseph Leroyer
St Jean Baptiste Badier

Sr Benedict Reynolds
Sr Victorine Pervez
Sr Winfrid Booth
Sr Winifred Hobin
Sr Teresa Lally
Sr Martha Darcy
Sr St Paul Brulay
Sr St Rose Rattingan
Sr St Vincent de Paul Mabire
Sr Stanislaus Lacey
Sr Ste Agnes Lebouteiller
Sr Ste Angele Corbin
Sr Ste Angele Lejemble
Sr Ste Anne Fretel
Sr Ste Blandine Cornely
Sr Ste Philomene Tencere
Sr Ste Philomene Tencere

Whilst every effort has been made to include every sister who has lived in England, we accept that due to limited early archives there may be some discrepancies

We wish to thank each and every one of our many contributors and well-wishers whose active support and encouragement has been invaluable throughout.

We would particularly like to express our gratitude to our Ursuline Sisters, past and present. Without them, this would not have been possible.

Una McCreesh OSU
Elizabeth Durrant
Compilers

Una McCreesh OSU   Elizabeth Durrant